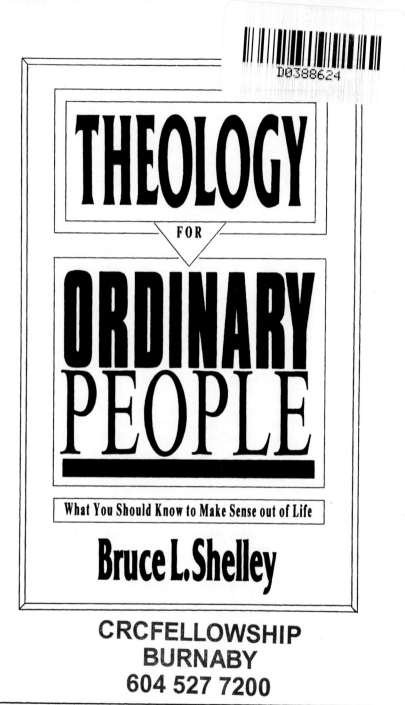

THEOLOGY

FOR

ORDINARY PEOPLE

What You Should Know to Make Sense out of Life

Bruce L. Shelley

CRCFELLOWSHIP
BURNABY
604 527 7200

INTERVARSITY PRESS
DOWNERS GROVE, ILLINOIS 60515

InterVarsity Press® is the book-publishing division of InterVarsity Christian Fellowship®, a student movement active on campus at hundreds of universities, colleges and schools of nursing in the United States of America, and a member movement of the International Fellowship of Evangelical Students. For information about local and regional activities, write Public Relations Dept., InterVarsity Christian Fellowship, 6400 Schroeder Rd., P.O. Box 7895, Madison, WI 53707-7895.

ISBN 0-8308-1342-X

Printed in the United States of America ∞

Library of Congress Cataloging-in-Publication Data

Shelley, Bruce L. (Bruce Leon), 1927-
    Theology for ordinary people: what you should know to make sense
out of life/ Bruce L. Shelley.
        p.   cm.
    Rev. ed. of: Christian theology in plain language. 1985.
    Includes bibliographical references and index.
    ISBN 0-8308-1342-X
    1. Theology, Doctrinal—Popular works.   2. Evangelicalism.
I. Shelley, Bruce L. (Bruce Leon), 1927-   Christian theology in
plain language.   II. Title.
BT77.S524   1993
230—dc20   92-34568
                                                                      CIP

17	16	15	14	13	12	11	10	9	8	7	6	5	4	3	2	1
07	06	05	04	03	02	01	00	99	98	97	96	95	94	93		

Foreword

A number of people have contributed to this book in special ways. It was originally published in 1985 by Word Books after Ernest Owen, then editorial director of Word, suggested the project over a warm breakfast one snowy December morning in Denver. The original title was *Christian Theology in Plain Language.* The present revision, new format and new title were made possible by the editors at InterVarsity Press. Rodney Clapp was especially helpful in indicating ways that the book could be improved.

The most obvious change throughout the chapters is the attempt to employ more inclusive language. Except in sentences where style and syntax would be damaged, I have tried to use *person, they* or *human nature* rather than *man, he* or *Man.* The practice proved most difficult in discussions of human nature where the traditional contrast "God and *Man"* seemed more direct and vivid than the indirect and abstract "God and *human nature"* or *"humanity."* In order to conserve the stylistic advantage, I have retained the traditional language in some contexts, but I hope my readers will recognize that I intend no sexist message.

Two of my students, Mark Smith and my son David Shelley, helped me in the early stages of several of the chapters. Then, at the other end of the process, two of my colleagues at Denver Seminary gave me the benefit of their insights. Robert L. Hubbard, professor of Old Testament, read the two chapters discussing the God who is above us and with us. And Professor James Cummings read the whole manuscript and offered many helpful suggestions. The last two chapters of the book—"The Final Curtain" and "New Day Dawning"—took on a special meaning for me when I learned that Jim had read them just hours after his doctor told him he had terminal cancer. He died in May 1985.

My editing and rewriting load was lightened considerably by Mrs. Denise Duke and Mrs. Doris Haslam, who took my disheveled manuscript and put it on diskettes while I was teaching in Brazil.

Words cannot express how deeply grateful I am for the help of all of these friends and to InterVarsity Press for this revised edition.

Bruce L. Shelley

Walking Together: An Introduction

Like many American families, ours has almost always had a dog to occupy the yard. Not only have the dogs been playful companions for our children, but they have also taught me a number of important lessons. Our last dog, Muffin, I discovered, had access to messages we human beings simply do not receive. She could be lying contentedly on our family-room floor, when suddenly she would jump to her feet and rush to the back door, only to return to the family room and look at us intently as though to say, "I want out of here, *now!*"

As soon as we opened the door, she would scamper toward the back fence, barking viciously. Why? She had heard some disturbing message beyond the range of human hearing. She knew some neighborhood cat had invaded her terrain. And out she went to defend her territory.

Modern scientists have created a host of devices for listening to this world beyond the frontier of human hearing: radio, sonar, radar, ultrasonics. These devices have become so much a part of modern travel, medicine and communications that we now take them for granted.

They should convince us all, however, that the world of our five senses is only a tiny part of reality.

This book is about another world, one beyond the range of all human senses, a world our secular society tries to ignore because we can't buy it or consume it or hoard it. Yet, as I hope to show, it is a world absolutely essential for any sort of meaningful life on planet earth. Let's just call it the Hidden World.

The book's cover, you will find, says nothing about the Hidden World. It speaks, instead, of the beliefs that Christians hold about reality—a set of beliefs called *theology*. Most people consider *theology* a scary term, rather like the names of the drugs a doctor prescribes for an infection. *Theology,* however, need not arouse our fears. It stands for something close to each of us, our religious convictions. It comes from two Greek words: *theos,* meaning God, and *logos,* rational thought. So theology is simply thinking about God and the Hidden World. And that is what we want to do in this book.

Let me explain what I mean by *theology*. I have in mind no more than what some people would call "the Christian faith." *Christian theology,* as I am using it, carries three basic ideas.

First, I mean the body of truth that Christians use to describe reality. Men and women who are looking for a sensible description of life and its meaning can find it in the Christian faith. It is understandable, it makes sense and it is true. Not everyone considers it so, I know. But that is what Christians have always claimed, and that is what I am trying to set forth in this book.

Second, Christian theology means the body of beliefs Christians have held for two thousand years, the historic faith. The Christian faith is not the peculiar convictions of a Christian believer here and there. Nor is it the exclusive property of a single Christian sect. It is the summation of the teachings of the Bible and the faith of the Christian church throughout the ages—it is what we call *catholic.*

Third, the Christian faith set forth in this book is my faith. I write not as an analyst; I write as a believer. Christian theology, as I understand it, is not only reasonable and catholic, it is also confessional.

So this book summarizes my faith. It is what the church has taught me and what I gladly confess.

In underscoring this confessional side of Christian theology, however, I do not want for a moment to suggest that this faith is my private possession in the same way that my attaché case or my desk lamp is mine. My faith is not mine in the sense that I have rights over it. I cannot tamper with it or toss it away. The Christian faith is mine only in the sense that I have accepted it as true. I have received it and have found that it has changed my life.

All this should indicate that this is not intended as another book on "basic Christian doctrine." I am not writing as a theologian to other theologians. My colleagues in theological circles know that I have neither the philosophical preparation nor the personal inclination to write such a book. I have in mind something less ambitious but more intimate. Throughout these chapters I have tried to imagine a long walk with a friend—a new Christian or a non-Christian—who has just asked me, "What do you mean by 'the Christian faith'?" So the book—I hope—is more like an extended personal conversation than the typical introductory course in theology.

In attempting to state the Christian faith plainly, I am not attempting to make it easy. I do not believe that is possible. Christianity is not easy to accept, easy to explore or easy to explain. That's because the gospel rests upon hard facts. The apostle Paul once said that the crucifixion of Jesus Christ was a scandal to the Jews of his day and foolishness to the Greeks. Today, men and women who confront the Christian faith for the first time often react in much the same way.

In our talk-show world, where one person's opinion seems to be as good as another's, people try to trace the gospel to the feelings of Christians. It is, they say, the way Christians have come to look at life. Other people, obviously, can look at it differently.

But that is not what Christians claim. They do not believe because they find the Christian faith easy. They believe because they find certain facts *hard.* The facts of the human condition, Jesus Christ's life and death, and the witness from the Hidden World are simply too compelling to resist. Christians confess that truths—hard facts—have overpowered them and gained control of their thinking and loyalties.

My intention is to present the Christian faith in a straightforward way, in a way that people without any formal theological training can understand. There are scores of well-written books about theology for Christians who have spent half of their lives in the church. What I wanted was a book that set forth the Christian faith for people who knew no theology. Such a person could be a new Christian or even a seeker who is interested in investigating the Christian faith without undue pressure to become a "convert."

To present the Christian faith to such people I chose a simple design. There are many ways to set forth Christianity. At times I think of it as a freshly baked pie. The cook usually slices the pie into pieces, so that the only difference in the servings is in size. The filling is the same throughout the pie. It doesn't matter where you begin to remove the pieces from the pie pan.

In the same way, Christian theology is, in one sense, a unified whole. You can slice it many ways and begin serving it from any of a number of points: the spiritual need of human beings, the character of God, the centrality of Jesus Christ or the basis of Christian beliefs.

I have chosen to pursue a narrative order. My story has a beginning, a sequence of events and a rather unpredictable climax. I chose this order because the Bible itself generally follows this sequence. We begin with a self-evident truth: most men and women who try to succeed in life without God encounter frustration, conflict and emptiness. Why? In spite of what we have heard, do we need faith after all?

We move on to push back the horizons of secular life and ask about the possibility of contact with another world, beyond the sights and sounds of day-to-day existence. Why do we have difficulty contacting that world? What does faith mean? Then we speak of the Ruler of that other realm and face the fact that he has already made contact with our world. His crucial message, it turns out, was communicated through a first-century Jewish teacher named Jesus Christ. As a result of Jesus' message, and death, and life beyond the grave, men and women can now find a new dimension to life, a new outlook upon their week-in-week-out world.

People made alive by contact with the Hidden World find their hopes and fears and labor dramatically changed because Jesus came. All who trust in him can look forward to a world beyond this life. Christ's people will someday enter that Hidden World where God is and discover directly and profoundly the meaning of "eternal life."

Summarized in this brief way, the Christian faith sounds like a cosmic myth. But it is no myth. Much of it has already happened, some of it is now unfolding and the best is yet to come. The point is that the Hidden World has contacted our world. Isaiah, the son of Amoz, spoke; Jesus of Nazareth lived; and the People of God endure. The faith is no myth. It is true.

This understanding of reality explains the tone you will find in this book. Since I believe that the Christian faith is true, I hold that other faiths are not fully true. They may be helpful to millions of people. They may be thought-provoking even to Christians. They may point toward the true faith. But since they are describing reality in another way, they are not true in the same sense that Christianity is true.

I intend no attack on these other faiths, be they non-Christian, counterfeit Christian or former Christian faiths. In order to make Christianity itself clear, I've resorted to some comparisons with these other faiths. I have tried to be fair in these comparisons. If I have failed in this attempt, I hope all non-Christians will recognize that my problem is ignorance, not disrespect.

Since I think that Christian theology should be catholic—a faith for all times and all people—I have also tried to avoid the emphases and teachings that are disputed among the major denominations in Christianity. I have convictions about some of these teachings myself. I am a Protestant, an evangelical and a Baptist; I can scarcely hide these facts. But I am also a student of Christian history. I know something of the differences within the catholic faith of all ages and the distinctive beliefs of the various traditions. In this book I haven't been able to avoid all references to these differences among Christians, but I've tried to subordinate these differences to the overriding purpose of setting forth the basic beliefs of Christians in all the denominations.

These pages will reveal some of my mentors in this faith. Among them are Augustine, Luther, Pascal, Edward John Carnell, C. S. Lewis, Harry Blamires, J. S. Whale, E. L. Mascall, P. T. Forsyth, Elton Trueblood, John R. W. Stott and many others. If I have been drawn to an author, I find it's usually because of an unusual insight into the way Christian truth touches human lives. These authors have a happy blend of head and heart. They have seen that genuine theology expresses itself in Christian living. I hope my readers will find that conviction reflected in these pages as well.

Now that we agree on the direction we want to go, let's get started on this hike.

1
LOST IN THE SECULAR CITY
THE HIDDEN WORLD

Not long ago my wife, Mary, and I visited a young friend in the hospital. She had just given birth to her first baby. When we arrived, Debbie was holding her tiny son. His little eyes blinked. He yawned just like an adult. His hairline and the shape of his nose reflected his father's rugged face. Little Lance was a living human being; no one could deny it.

During our visit, Debbie said to us, "You know, it was so strange. One minute there were three of us in the delivery room. And the next, there were four." It was her way of describing the wonder of life. Her baby had brought her to the frontier of the Hidden World. What, she asked, is the meaning of life?

The Secular Gospel
The secular world in which Debbie's baby will grow up finds no mystery in his birth and no ultimate purpose in his life, and it provides no hope for his hour of death. According to today's secular faith, Lance is a creature of one world. That world has three conditions in

which he will live: space, time and matter. Beyond that, nothing! There is no Hidden World to explain his mother's wonder or to direct his life on planet earth. Secularism simply ignores all clues to another world.

Today, especially in Western Europe and North America, the relentless projection of secularism's image of reality makes any clear painting of the Christian faith a difficult undertaking. Christianity holds that human beings are unique creatures on planet earth. They have the potential for contact with another realm of life, a spiritual world of fulfillment and permanence. But the promoters of Western secularism say human beings are simply highly sexed animals who live only for the prestige and pleasures of this life.

This secular view of human nature is part of a strange gospel. The high priests of secularism tell us that we can find personal fulfillment by accumulating more and more things. The steps to success and happiness are rather clear. You go to college; you get a car; you try out several mates and settle on one; then you buy a house. You work hard—or find the right shortcuts—and you get a significant raise in pay. Then you can move up to a bigger house and buy a better car, always sustained by faith in the promises of the advertisers.

It is a cozy picture. The sun always shines; people always smile. The nearest thing to pain is the arrival of the bills to pay for it all. The only hint that it may end someday is the promise that you will be cushioned by the retirement programs of the welfare state. That is the sum of life's meaning and purpose: things, pleasure, security and rest. All in this life.

This secular view of life carries two consequences. First, nothing after death need concern us. If secular men and women think of life after death at all, their thoughts are almost certainly positive. Traditional images of judgment and hell only remain in our society as subjects for laughter. Second, nothing in life need trouble us except the things of this world. God, devils, prayer and grace play no part in the secular gospel.

Obviously, such a gospel creates an unconscious bias against the

Hidden World. No one escapes the incessant propaganda of the secular faith. So we grow up conditioned to scoff at ideas of any reality beyond the dimensions of the natural world.

Will Herberg, the Jewish scholar, once argued that this social brainwashing was a far more important cause of contemporary unbelief than any rational argument from atheism. "What has affected the modern mind," he said, "has not been an array of intellectual arguments, but the unremitting operation of mind-setting attitudes, often hardly noticed, doing their remorseless work by cultural pressures and compulsions."[1]

Life Without Meaning

A number of signs indicate that the proverbial baby has vanished with the bath water. Secular people are left without any ultimate meaning in life. Can material things really satisfy the hunger of the soul? Will constant care of the body fulfill the needs of the spirit?

The question is worth pressing, because one of the striking features of today's secular society is moral anarchy—violence, sensuality, dishonesty, crime. I am not suggesting that we ought to encourage religion in order to get people to behave. My point lies in another direction. If the secular gospel were really what it is touted to be—a guarantee of contentment and happiness—why all the restlessness and rage?

Christians are not alone in pointing out this contemporary bewilderment. The bafflement of the modern soul is one of the recurring themes in twentieth-century novels and plays. Franz Kafka, D. H. Lawrence, Henry Miller and Samuel Beckett would never be accused of harboring Christian prejudices, and yet they speak powerfully of the emptiness of men and women without faith.[2]

Similar testimony comes from internationally known psychiatrists. Carl Jung once said, "The central neurosis of our time is emptiness." A supporting diagnosis came from Viktor Frankl, who said that "clinics are crowded with people suffering from a new kind of neurosis, a sense of total and ultimate meaninglessness of life." The frustration comes because men and women have an "inherent tendency to reach out for meanings to fulfill and values to actualize."

No physician, however, has diagnosed the sickness of the soul without faith any more profoundly than the ancient Hebrew author of Ecclesiastes. He personally sought satisfaction in sensual pleasures, in elaborate houses and in pursuit of knowledge. And what did he find? He hated life. He discovered that all the good things of this life only lead to disillusionment. Everything, he says, is "meaningless, a chasing after the wind" (Eccl 1:14).

Writers of our time have produced many stories of men and women who have lost their sense of identity. Some accident, perhaps some blow to the head, has driven them into amnesia, and they must wander about the countryside in search of an answer to the maddening question "Who am I?" Outwardly they look like everyone else, but they are lost and confused, desperate to know who they are and where they belong.

Early in this century, the witty British journalist G. K. Chesterton said that this is the story of every one of us. We have all forgotten who we are. And without some help in finding our true identity, we haven't much of an idea what we should be doing.[3]

The Religious Quest

That is the fallacy of the secular faith. It simply does not fit the facts of human existence. It asks us to believe that nonrational nature has managed to produce a race of creatures who ask, "What's behind it all?"

A survey of ancient cultures and contemporary tribes indicates that belief in gods or a God is a very common thing. A person who completely denies the Hidden World and insists that there is no purposeful cause behind the universe is a rare creature. Throughout the history of humankind, the vast majority of people on planet earth have looked for some purpose behind everything. They have sensed that there is more to life than they can see. Someone, or a host of someones, is over us and around us. And since we are surrounded by this greater world, we will have to give an account for the way we have lived on this planet. There must be some life after death.

When people entertain thoughts like these, they are on their way to a religious quest of meaning, because religion is the refusal to believe that the universe can be adequately explained in three-dimensional terms.

The fact that there are several rival sets of beliefs about the unseen world does not mean that all of them are wrong and that one of them cannot be right. If, as Christianity teaches, the Maker has created human beings in his own image to have fellowship with him, then it isn't surprising if people all over the world and through all the ages have tried to find him.

Once, when the early Christian leader Paul was visiting Athens, he stood before a gathering of the Areopagus and said: "Men of Athens! I see that in every way you are very religious. . . . The God who made the world and everything in it . . . gives all men life and breath and everything else. From one man he made every nation of men, . . . and he determined the times set for them and the exact places where they should live. God did this so that men would seek him and perhaps reach out for him and find him, though he is not far from each one of us" (Acts 17:22-27).

To identify the Hidden World, the German scholar Rudolf Otto coined the term *the numinous*. It comes to us, he said, under the dual guise of the terrible and the attractive, awakening in us either awe or delight. The birth of Debbie's baby was obviously a delight. The sudden appearance of a funnel cloud over Kansas can produce a sense of awe. In either case, Christians believe that the Hidden World is real, and they try to understand who is there and what he wants of us.

Such a view of reality rejects secularism and calls for another starting point for the human quest. If secularism proves a dead end, we have no alternative. We must go back and head in another direction.

In one of his books G. B. Caird, the Oxford professor, tells the story of a yokel who was stopped by a passing traveler and asked, "How can I get to Cambridge from here?"

"If I was going to Cambridge," said the yokel, "I wouldn't start from here."[4]

Sometimes our starting point is all wrong. So our best move is to look for a new one. Instead of denying the Hidden World, suppose we look for it. Then, where will we find it?

Some world religions counsel us to flee this world of time, space and matter if we want to find the Hidden World. "There is a state of being beyond this life," they say. "God lives there and there you must seek the Great Spirit." In other words, we must flee from this world if we want to find the Hidden World. This is the counsel of many Eastern religions and recent voices for the "New Age."

Remarkably, however, this is not Christianity's counsel. It agrees that the Hidden World exists and God is there, but it also asserts that God himself has visited our world of time, space and matter. He became one of us. He demonstrated that life in our passing world can be incorporated into his eternal life and that this life can be a genuine prelude for the life to come.

The Image of God

A clue to understanding this intersection of two worlds lies in human nature. In some ways men and women are no different than other species upon the earth. We share space, time and matter with many other creatures. But in other ways humanity stands out from all the rest. According to the Bible's description of human nature, men and women stand out, not primarily by what they can do, but by what they are. They are made in "the image of God." We learn something about an artist from his paintings, and something about a legislator from his laws, and something about a parent from his children. So we discover something about God in human nature.

Christians have often debated the meaning of that "image." It is probably not limited to a single characteristic, but at the heart of its meaning is the special capacity to live in a personal relationship with God.

In the story of creation in the Bible we read that Adam walked and talked with God. They were able to communicate personally with one another. On the one hand, man could communicate with God: he could worship him and thank him. And on the other hand, God could speak to Adam. He could explain his purposes and plans for him. The "image of God" in human nature, then, means the power to love and serve the Maker and his other children.

Today, we know that men and women do not do this well or often. Something has apparently gone wrong with the original plan. And if a thing fails in its essential purpose, its very existence is endangered. A fire that does not burn is not a fire. Men and women, however, reveal their restlessness about their failure.

"Do fish complain of the sea for being wet?" C. S. Lewis once asked. "Or if they did, would the fact not strongly suggest that they had not always been, or would not always be, purely aquatic creatures? If you are really a product of a material universe, how is it that you don't feel at home there?" Humans' hunger, said Lewis, does not prove that they will be fed. They may starve, but surely their hunger says that their bodies need food and that it comes from a world where the stuff exists.[5]

Christians find reflections of this smudged image of God in several human characteristics. Men and women, for example, have a sense of obligation. They seem to think it matters how they live. Somewhere, people have gotten the idea that certain attitudes and actions are right and others are wrong. They even teach these ideas to their children. And the strangest thing is that so many people can give no rational explanation for these ideas. They just know that human beings should not harm those who are kindest to them, or steal an elderly woman's last few dollars, or beat children or do any of the many other things that contradict ideas of justice, decency and fair play.

We even make laws to try to keep others from violating these standards. Every now and then you hear someone say, "You can't legislate morality." But that is a ridiculous statement: nearly all legislation is aimed at protecting moral standards. They are basic to human existence.

Even when people are acting most like animals, they know that they are special creatures. Think of the contrasts with our furry friends. No one thinks of stopping an alley cat from clawing another one by saying, "Hey, take it easy!" But a man who through careless driving maims another person feels guilty. He knows what he did is not what he should have done.

Of course, people do break these standards, and they may well try to excuse themselves or argue that the rule they broke was not all that important. But as soon as someone else wrongs them, they appeal to the same moral standards, protesting that the action against them was wrong or unfair. The atheistic scientist will still deny another person's right to steal her property.

And where did people get this sense of obligation? Are we to believe that some body fluid produces it? Or is it a reflection of the One who created men and women? Isn't that what we should expect? If people are in any way in the likeness of their Creator, their moral sense should reflect it. That, at any rate, is what the Bible suggests. It says when people without a written moral code—"Gentiles"—"do by nature the things required by the law, . . . they show that the requirements of the law are written on their hearts" (Rom 2:14-15).

Or consider another human trait, a kind of spiritual bond with nature. Why, for example, are human beings moved by unusual experiences? We can analyze music in terms of vibrations and acoustics, but we cannot explain its effect on the human soul. We experience more than some scientific reaction when we watch crashing waves, or smell the smoke of pine logs burning, or feel the breeze that wafts through the oak leaves.

"It is," wrote J. B. Phillips, "as though there was another dimension. . . . We may well begin to suspect that this physical world is in fact shot through and through with spiritual realities." Humans seem to sense that spiritual dimension.[6]

Christians hold, then, that these special human qualities are clues to life's purpose, memories of a kingdom long gone. "Who is unhappy at not being a king," the seventeenth-century genius Blaise Pascal once asked, "except a deposed king? All of these miseries of man prove man's greatness. They are the miseries of a deposed king." His point was well taken. People are born into royalty but they have been expelled from the kingdom. They are children of God but have lost contact with their Father.

We can understand, then, why little Lance's birth was for Debbie more than a routine experience. It was a personal pointer to the Hidden World, and the heavenly Father's house.

2
WE ARE
NOT ALONE
REVELATION

Out of the depths of his agony Job, an ancient Near Eastern patriarch, sobbed,

If only I knew where to find him;
    if only I could go to his dwelling!
I would state my case before him
    and fill my mouth with arguments.
I would find out what he would answer me,
    and consider what he would say. (Job 23:3-5)

This ancient tragedy, the story of Job's losses of property and health and family, is a striking reminder of the fact that our human horizons are too narrow to provide a satisfying view of life and its sorrows. There is something profoundly Christian about Job's discovery that human wisdom alone offers no adequate explanation of life's meaning.

In one sense men and women are never prepared to hear from the Hidden World until they have discovered secularism's silence. "If only I knew where to find God!"

People, it seems, share a universal concern: How can I contact reality? Where can I find God?

The world teems with religions, each of them offering some explanation of the human quest for life's meaning. We can reduce this number, however, to three basic views: atheism, pantheism and theism.

Basic Religious Views

The first view, atheism, says no God exists. Humanity's belief in God is a figment of the human imagination. Men and women, says the atheist, invented the term *God* in order to explain those mysteries in life that they could not fathom.

The British philosopher Bertrand Russell once intoned the atheist's creed in his unique style. An atheist, he confessed, believes "that man is the product of causes which had no prevision of the end they were achieving; that his origin, his growth, his hopes and fears, his loves and beliefs, are but the outcome of accidental collocations of atoms; that no fire, no heroism, no intensity of thought or feeling, can preserve an individual life beyond the grave; that all the labor of the ages, all the devotion, all the inspiration, all the noonday brightness of human genius, are destined to extinction in the vast death of the solar system."[1]

Such a creed needs no word from God. There is no God to speak. So how do men and women find reality?

Many atheists accept the religion of humanism. Humanists find nothing in the universe to worship; they call instead for a special reverence for Man. (And they insist on the capitalization of the term.) They believe that people can invest their passing existence with meaning if they will rely upon the powers of reason, including science and education, to create and attain self-improvement and social progress for humankind.

For almost three hundred years human reason has reigned in the Western world, as David Hume, the eighteenth-century philosopher, once said, "prescribing laws and imposing maxims, with an absolute sway." In intellectualized religions, such as humanism, this "god" judges truth and life itself by the laws of logical consistency. Reality must bow before the throne of the human mind.

As Hume himself acknowledged, however, reason alone can never demonstrate its right to rule. Men and women are merely finite beings. Their grasp of reality is too small. They will never generate sufficient wisdom to answer the questions of the universe or to understand reality's fullness.

The second fundamental view of reality is pantheism. Unlike atheism, which finds God nowhere, pantheism finds God everywhere. Its distinctive belief is summed up in its name, from two Greek words. *Pan* means all and *theos* means God. So to pantheists "God is all and all is God." In other words, pantheists identify God with the universe and the universe with God. Pantheists, therefore, do *not* believe in a God who has an existence apart from the world and who chose to create the universe by his own powerful Word.

One primitive form of pantheism, accepted today by 100 million people in Africa, Asia and Latin America, is animism. An animist believes that the natural world is filled with spirits or gods. Like their ancestors before them, animists sense intuitively some power above or beyond them and their world.

Their fathers were so often subject to the forces of nature—wind and fire and rain—that they often personified and deified these powers. When rains flooded their fields, they took their misfortune to be the angry voice of the rain god. The best course seemed to lie in appeasing his wrath. So they brought to the angry spirit an offering or a sacrifice. When rains fell gently, bringing a welcome harvest, animists believed that the rain god had shown his favor and that they should respond with thanksgiving.

This line of thinking filled pantheons in ancient Greece and groves in Canaan. But these gods do not fully answer the human dilemma. They may address the powers of nature—they may even give the worshiper a sense of oneness with the universe—but they do not give life meaning. They lack a reference point outside the painful passage of time. They do not satisfy Job's search for a word of comfort from a

God out there who can hear his complaint.

Think of the pantheist's life as a ship at sea. On board it is impossible to tell how fast the ship is moving by looking either at the surging water or at the furniture on the deck. Moving with the tide, the ship seems to cut through the ocean effortlessly, while in fact it is speeding through the waves. When the ship sails against the current, the opposite is true. The waters move swiftly by, but the ship makes little progress. It is impossible to know the ship's actual speed without some fixed point, some North Star, to serve as a point of reference.

Spiritual reality is the same. As long as we search inside ourselves or in the world about us, we will never find the answers to our questions about meaning. We need some fixed point outside our world.

Christians—and others who hold the third view of reality, theism—believe that reality's North Star is a message from the Hidden World. The Creator of heaven and earth has not left men and women to die in Russell's cosmic silence. He has spoken to us. He has chosen to disclose his purpose to human beings. Job's question, then, is not the appropriate one to ask. The real question is not "How can we find God?" It is, rather, "How has God revealed himself to us?"

When Christians consider the ways God speaks to us, they recognize two types of communication: one through his world and the other through his Word. They call these general revelation and special revelation. The two differ in their audiences and in their aims.

General revelation is given to all people of all times. It is the fingerprint of God left on the works of creation. Special revelation is given to specific people at specific times. It is a message from God explaining his purpose in a special segment of history. General revelation indicates that God exists but that men and women refuse to honor him as a generous Creator. Special revelation does more. It discloses God's character, his plans for human beings and his saving works. It calls men and women to repentance and faith in God.

"All men have the general knowledge," the Protestant reformer Martin Luther once said. "But what God thinks of us, what he wants to give and do to deliver us from sin and death and to save us—this men do not know. Thus it can happen that someone's face may be familiar to me but I do not really know him, because I do not know what he has in his mind. So it is that men know naturally that there is a God, but they do not know what he wants and what he does not want."[2]

God's Familiar Face

We find God's general revelation in his creation. The natural order—the world of sights and smells and sounds—is filled with hints and clues of the presence and power of God: the lightning flash, the spider's web, the galaxy's order. These and countless other impressions from the universe are whispers of the God who made them all. The ancient Hebrews sang of this wonder:

The heavens declare the glory of God;

the skies proclaim the work of his hands. (Ps 19:1)

Paul, the early Christian evangelist, agreed. Since the creation of the world, he said, "God's invisible qualities—his eternal power and divine nature—have been clearly seen." Men and women detect these qualities in the things God has made (Rom 1:18-20).

The tribespeople of Ecuador and Indonesia, then, are not entirely misled in fearing the spirits of the forests and streams. The visible world does veil an invisible one. Their sin, like our own, lies in worshiping and serving created things rather than the Creator. The brush strokes of nature are designed to introduce us to the Artist. He set us in the world of wonders, not to make us idolaters, but to make us thankful.

Of all the things that God has made, none carries his image quite like human creatures. The power of reason, by which men and women question God's existence, is itself a sign of God's handiwork. As we have said, reason alone is ill-equipped to sit in judgment of God's truth. That is impossible. No human mind is capable of that. But our ability to think at all is a reflection of God's character. He is no irrational force. He is the Source of all reason. If that were not so we could never understand his self-disclosure.

Without reason, we have no basis for insisting that one faith is any better or any worse than another. All talk of God or religion would be so much meaningless babbling. But if God is rational, then we may expect his message to us to be reasonable.

In the end, then, the general revelation from God discloses the human potential; it does not solve the human problem. Men and women know enough to confess that they do not know. This general revelation shows that people have longings they cannot satisfy because they are made for a homeland they have fled. "Our lifelong nostalgia," C. S. Lewis once said, "to be on the inside of some door which we have always seen from the outside, is no mere neurotic fancy, but the truest index of our real situation."[3]

The Authority of the Bible
The Christian faith, however, holds that God has chosen to speak to human beings not only through creation but also through a special stream of human history recorded in the Bible. We call this "special revelation" because it carries a special message from God to the ancient people Israel and to their spiritual heirs in the Christian church.

That claim, I know, sparks a powder keg of questions: How can the eternal God be revealed in and through human history? How can time carry the message of eternity? God, by common understanding, is universal, and history is the story of particular events. The very expression "historical revelation" borders on the absurd.

Christians have never denied the difficulty. The apostle Paul once said that the preaching of the cross was "foolishness to Gentiles" (1 Cor 1:23). Men and women would never have dreamed of such a story. It is only because the story actually happened that Christians ever got the idea of preaching it.

In other words, the inscrutable God who inhabits eternity has himself bridged the chasm into time. He decided to communicate with men and women in the way they can understand—through human history. The omnipresent and eternal God made himself known in the temporal process. One special segment of history became his channel of communication and reached a climax in his ultimate message: "The Word became flesh and lived for a while among us" (Jn 1:14)—perhaps the most astonishing statement in the whole Bible.

When the Bible uses the expression "the Word of God" it intends what Christians call "God's *revelation,*" the words or actions of God through which he makes himself known to men and women.

We read that by his Word, God created the heavens and the earth. "By the word of the Lord were the heavens made, their starry host by the breath of his mouth" (Ps 33:6). God also spoke to the Hebrew prophets. Their constant claim was "the word of the Lord came to me." Finally, in "the last days" he spoke through Jesus Christ, his special Son (Heb 1:1-2). By announcing this revelation of God, Christians make spiritual life available to those who believe the message. Men and women find genuine faith in the way they "hear" the Word and gain new life by its power (Rom 10:17).

According to the Bible, the Word of God—this lively revelation from God—is both an event within human history and an explanation of its meaning. Put another way, the Word is both an act of God and an utterance of God. For example, it is both the exodus of Israel from Egypt and the law given to the Israelite people at Mount Sinai. It possesses an element of power along with an element of truth. The Word has the unique ability to bring persons face to face with the Living God and to hold them accountable for their life before God.

We call this power to demand human obedience *divine authority.* In ordinary life we settle disputes by appealing to an authority. It may be a book of law, a medical journal or a flight schedule. In any case, an authority possesses the power to settle an issue. So in matters about God and his relationships with men and women, the authority is the Word of God.

Christians have always believed that the Scriptures—first the Old Testament alone, then the New Testament added—share in this authority. They are more than a mere record of the Word of God. They *are* the Word of God in the sense that they too convey the message of God's acts, and they act upon the souls of men and women and call for a response to God. It's not possible for scholars to extract somehow the great truths from the history of Israel or from Jesus' teaching in order to create general religious principles for humanity and then discard the biblical events as so many myths. Truth is in the biblical story and power is in its telling. That is why the Bible sets the standard for beliefs in Christianity.

Obviously, men and women can read the Bible simply as ancient Hebrew literature. They do it all the time. But when Christians speak of the Bible as the Word of God, they are talking about what C. S. Lewis once called "getting the focus right." It is possible, he said, for a person to contend that a poem is nothing but black marks on white paper. And such an argument might be convincing before an audience that could not read. You could examine the print under a microscope or analyze the paper and ink, but this sort of analysis would never reveal anything that you could call "a poem." Those who can read, however, will continue to insist that poems exist.[4]

One of the terms Christians use to describe this special focus of the Bible is *inspiration*. This is a well-worn word in English. A soccer team, we say, played an inspired game against a stronger opponent. Or we might try to explain to a friend the inspiration we felt during the playing of Tchaikovsky's *1812 Overture*. In this use of the word we mean an exalting or elevating state. No doubt the biblical prophets and apostles had these inspired moments.

Christians, however, mean more than that in speaking of the Bible's inspiration. They mean that the Bible came to the writers as a result of God's initiative, not any human plan. That, at any rate, is what the Bible itself often says about the writings of the prophets and apostles.

The idea of inspiration, though not the word, appears in a rather well-known passage in 2 Timothy 3:16. It says Scripture was "God-breathed," a Hebrew way of saying that something was produced by the power or energy of God.

Another passage, 2 Peter 1:20-21, uses a different image for God's activity. It says the prophets of God were "carried along" by God's Spirit, like a ship propelled by winds filling its sails. Inspiration, then, stands for all the activities of God in selecting, moving and imparting his Word to the prophets of the Old Testament and to the apostles of the New in the course of their writing the Scriptures. This activity of God seldom overwhelmed the authors. They were not carried away into a mystical world of heavenly truths. They retained their individuality, with styles and perspectives uniquely their own. Some were scholars; others were peasants. Some were rural; others were urban. Each brought personal vocabulary, temperament and experience to the special work of communicating the Word.

As a consequence, Christians hold that the Bible is both a divine and a human book. It communicates the Word of God, yet it calls for study like any other piece of literature. It is both the Word of God and the words of people. It demands submission and faith; but at the same time it requires study and interpretation.

"If God does speak in Scripture," some may be inclined to ask, "then what language does he use?" My answer is in the story about a woman who took up Hebrew in her advanced years because she wanted to be able to greet her Maker in his native tongue. The question, I fear, is taking a biblical figure of speech to a humorous extreme.

The Bible often speaks of the spiritual realities of the Hidden World. In order to make these realms intelligible to us it employs symbolic or metaphorical language. And that too poses a troublesome problem for many people. If we take these expressions literally, as the elderly woman did, they will mislead us. We use no scales to measure the weight of an argument and no mathematics to calculate the height of a lofty ideal. We never get a suntan from the glow of a sunny disposition or the illumination of a brilliant scholar. In day-to-day conversation we seem to manage metaphors quite well. Why should we have so much trouble understanding the Bible?

Some people, when they recognize a biblical metaphor, tend to dilute the image to some vapid moralism. They have the good sense to recognize that "hellfire" is a metaphor, but they unwisely conclude that it means nothing more serious than inward remorse, something we often experience this side of the grave. Or they rightly think that the apostle spoke metaphorically when he said Christians are "raised" to "walk in newness of life" (Rom 6:4 KJV); but they misunderstand him completely if they think he meant the Christian faith consists of nothing more than a respectable life in acceptable society.

This type of interpretation is so common that it creates a distinct impression that some people do not have trouble with biblical metaphors so much as with biblical miracles. And if that is true, then these people will never understand the Bible or Christianity. If you subtract the miraculous elements from Hindu pantheism, all the essential beliefs remain. The same is obviously true of humanism, since humanism by definition leaves no room for miracles. But a Christianity without miracles is not Christianity. It is something else.

Job came to see that. At one point in his depression he looked for God in order to state his case. But when he finally encountered the Lord, he learned that in the presence of God a man does not fill his mouth with words, but with wonder.

3

THE EXODUS
AND THE ENTRANCE
THE BIBLE

In A.D. 303, when it was still illegal to be a Christian, the Roman emperor Diocletian issued a decree that he hoped would extinguish the spreading flames of Christianity. The primary objective of the mandate was the seizure and destruction of the Christian Scriptures.

Later that year, officials enforced the decree in North Africa. One of the targets was a man named Felix, bishop of Tibjuca, a village near Carthage. The mayor of the town ordered Felix to hand over his Scriptures. Though some judges were willing to accept mere scraps of parchment, Felix refused to surrender the Word of God at the insistence of mere men. Resolutely, he resisted compromise.

The Roman authorities finally shipped Felix to Italy, where he paid for his stubbornness with his life. On August 30, as the record puts it, "with pious obstinacy" he laid down his life rather than surrender his Gospels.[1]

In our day when the Bible is so readily available we may find Felix's dogged determination mystifying. It does highlight, however, a fact of central importance for understanding the Christian faith: Christianity is inextricably linked to the Bible. All its basic affirmations arise from the story of the ancient people of Israel and their most controversial offshoot, the Jesus movement. We may justifiably ask, then, what is the Bible all about?

At first glance the Bible is a strange sort of book. It contains sixty-six smaller books, written by approximately forty authors over a period of sixteen hundred years. The first thirty-nine books, called the Old Testament, were originally Jewish Scriptures and were written mostly in Hebrew. The twenty-seven books called the New Testament were written later by Christians in Greek.

The Old Testament is often divided into the Law (the first five books), the Prophets and the Writings, which include the popular Psalms and Proverbs. The New Testament can also be divided into the Gospels (four of them) and the Epistles (or letters). The Acts of the Apostles serves as a historical bridge from the Gospels to the Epistles, and the last book, Revelation, provides a unique climax to the whole collection.

The thread running through the sixty-six books is the story of human rebellion against God, the Creator, and God's merciful acts intended to elicit repentance and faith in men and women. The story is no myth. It really happened. That is one reason we say Christianity is a historical religion. God's message about himself and his reconciliation of rebellious human beings is an unfolding history of a nation called Israel and a person called Jesus. The Christian faith cannot be divorced from this biblical story.

Biblical history, however, is not identical with our modern view of history. A modern historian is supposed to give an objective account of the facts of his or her period. Biblical history, however, is *interpreted history*. Biblical authors have a point of view. They share a testimony as well as tell a story.

The authors were selective, therefore, in their choice of material. Rather than focus on the movements of the mighty ancient empires—Assyria, Babylon, Persia, Egypt, Greece and Rome—they mentioned these only as they impinged on the relatively inconsequential Israelite communities in Palestine. The Bible isn't concerned with the wisdom, wealth or might of this world, but with the salvation provided by God.

The Start of the Story

The story begins with time itself: "In the beginning God created the heavens and the earth." And on the sixth day of creation the Lord God crowned his work by fashioning men and women "in his own image." When God checked on his handiwork, he saw that it was very good— but not for long. Only three chapters into the story, human beings stumble into moral ruin. The rest of the Bible is about the rescue of the rebels.

After the initial sin of the original pair, Adam and Eve, their children plunged into the grossest immorality. God even came to regret that he had made the human pair, so he decided to destroy the earth by a flood. With an eye on the future, however, he arranged for the survival of a single household—Noah and his family.

Even this dreadful judgment failed to cure men and women of their depravity. Noah's descendants took the same path as Adam and Eve. In their pride they refused to accept the Lord as God and to worship him.

As a result, somewhere around 2000 B.C., God decided to implement a new strategy in his dealings with men and women. He turned to a specific people who became his new beachhead in the world.

A nation began with a single man, Abraham. While living in Ur of the Chaldees (ancient Mesopotamia and modern Iraq), Abraham heard God's call: "Leave your country, your people and your father's household and go to the land I will show you." Then God offered Abraham a promise. "I will make you into a great nation and I will bless you. . . . I will bless those who bless you, and whoever curses you I will curse; and all peoples on earth will be blessed through you" (Gen 12:1-3). The remainder of the Bible is the unfolding of this promise, called the *covenant*.

Abraham passed on this promise to his son, Isaac, born to Abraham and Sarah when they were beyond their childbearing years. Then Isaac repeated the promise to his son Jacob, whose name was also Israel. Finally, Jacob passed the promise to his twelve sons, the heads of the twelve tribes of Israel.

Through the treachery of his brothers, Joseph, one of Israel's sons, was sold into slavery in Egypt. But, as Joseph himself put it, what his brothers intended for evil, God intended for good. Joseph the slave became Joseph the vice pharaoh, his authority second only to the power of the pharaoh (or king) of Egypt. When a famine struck Canaan, Jacob and his family moved to Egypt, where Joseph provided all their needs. For 430 years Israel's descendants flourished and multiplied in Egypt.

Joseph probably came to power during the reign of the Hyksos rulers (about 1700 B.C.), the foreign "shepherd kings" who ruled between Egyptian dynasties. These favorable years ended, however, when "a new king arose over Egypt who did not know Joseph" (Ex 1:8 NASB). This new pharaoh, perhaps Rameses II, conscripted the Hebrews into labor camps and stone quarries. And the people of Israel cried out to God for deliverance; "and God heard their groaning, and God remembered his covenant with Abraham" (Ex 2:24 RSV).

Deliverance came from an unexpected source, Pharaoh's own palace. After training in the royal courts and enduring lonely years in the Sinai wilderness, Moses was ready to fulfill his destiny. He heard the call from the Lord and delivered God's message to Pharaoh: "Let my people go." Pharaoh's determined resistance provoked God to send a series of plagues, the last one killing all the firstborn sons in Egypt except those of the Hebrews. Jews still celebrate this event in the Passover holiday. Pharaoh's resistance finally crumbled. He let the people go.

The Israelites were hardly on the road when Pharaoh reverted to his former stubbornness and pursued the bedraggled band of ex-slaves. With the sea before them and Egyptian troops closing in behind, the Israelites watched as Moses stretched out his staff and the sea parted.

We do not know the exact location of the "Red Sea"—as the King

James Bible translated it—or the "Sea of Reeds," as the Hebrew Bible says. But we do know that the water was deep enough to drown a battalion of Egyptian soldiers, and to splash the exodus forever across Hebrew memory.

The Covenant at Sinai

The ragged multitude of grumbling Israelites eventually reached the foot of Mount Sinai, where Moses had met the Lord at a burning bush years before. Here God gave Israel three special gifts: the renewed covenant, a moral law and an atoning sacrifice.

The covenant came first. "You have seen what I did to the Egyptians," God told Israel, "and how I bore you on eagles' wings and brought you to myself. Now, therefore, if you will obey my voice and keep my covenant, you shall be my own possession among all peoples" (Ex 19:4-5 RSV). The people happily accepted God's covenant.

Keeping this covenant meant obeying God's moral law. Its essence was the Ten Commandments, which gave Israel the essentials for maintaining a right relationship with God and with people.

But what if the Israelites broke the moral law? That was the purpose of the sacrificial system and the ceremonial law. Every dramatic action of the system carried some message and looked forward to that final, once-for-all sacrifice of the Perfect Lamb that God would one day offer.

With the law in hand, the chosen people headed for their promised land. When they reached the border of Palestine, however, they halted in faithless fear. The inhabitants of the land seemed like giants to them. The Israelites' unbelief provoked the Lord. He condemned his people to wandering in the wilderness until every adult of that generation perished. Only after forty years, under the leadership of Joshua, did the people of promise enter the land of promise.

Joshua's first responsibility as leader of the Israelites was the conquest of the local inhabitants, the Canaanites. After a series of military victories, Joshua parceled out the land to the twelve tribes of Israel. But he failed to subdue the local populations. As a result, the

Canaanites persisted as a constant source of political and religious irritation.

The book of Judges illustrates this repeatedly. Time and again the Israelites succumbed to the worship of Baal and Ashtaroth, the local Canaanite fertility gods. The Lord would respond by allowing an oppressor to gain the upper hand over one of the tribes. When the people called on the Lord for deliverance, he would send a judge, a military leader, to break the bonds of the oppressor.

After two hundred years of such ups and downs, and especially the defeat at the hands of the Philistines, the Israelites had had enough. They cried out for a king, "that we also may be like all the nations" (1 Sam 8:20 RSV).

The Age of Kings (1050-586 B.C.)

God complied with the Israelites' request and gave them a king. They chose Saul, the strongest, most handsome man in Israel. Though Saul was somewhat successful in his military exploits, he was not always content to obey the Lord. Three times he specifically disregarded direct commands of God. His downfall began when a young shepherd boy named David won the praise of Israel by defeating the Philistine hero Goliath. Wild with jealousy, Saul spent his last years as king haplessly hounding David, the anointed heir to his throne.

Whereas Saul was a king by popular choice, David was a king by God's choice. Under David's dynamic leadership, Israel subdued its enemies and extended its borders: from the "river of Egypt" (Egypt's frontier wadi extending into the Sinai) to the River Euphrates in Mesopotamia.

David was more than an ancient warlord. He was also an artist— a musician in Saul's court. He had a sensitive spirit, and he was generous with his enemies and loyal to his friends. Above all, he was devoted to the Lord. Aside from his tragic sin against Bathsheba and Uriah, his life was marked by exceptional piety. The psalms he wrote reveal an unsurpassed depth of spirituality.

As he had with Moses, God renewed his covenant with David. But this time he added a new note: the permanence of the Davidic throne. "Your house and your kingdom shall be made sure for ever before me" (2 Sam 7:16 RSV). This became the keynote of Israel's hope for the next four hundred years. God would sustain the Davidic line until the ultimate triumph of Messiah, the special leader in Israel's future.

David was succeeded by his son Solomon. Gifted with unusual wisdom, Solomon brought Israel to a zenith of economic prosperity, peace and strength. Unfortunately, he achieved much of his success by conscripted labor. Solomon's major weakness, however, was women. In defiance of the Lord's prohibition of intermarriage, he kept a harem of foreign princesses, and they "turned his heart after other gods" (1 Kings 11:4).

Rehoboam, Solomon's son, inherited his father's troubles as well as his throne. People of the north of Israel, who had groaned under Solomon's oppressive measures, demanded a reprieve from Rehoboam. The king replied with threats of a heavier yoke for the necks of such grumblers. He succeeded in provoking the northern ten tribes into seceding from the Davidic dynasty. After 120 years, the kingdom of Israel was irreparably split. Only the tribes of Judah and Benjamin remained loyal to the throne established by God's covenant.

A former government official named Jeroboam assumed the leadership of the northern kingdom, sometimes called Israel, sometimes called Ephraim. He faced problems immediately. The temple that Solomon had built was in Jerusalem, Rehoboam's capital. If Jeroboam's subjects made pilgrimages there, he was bound to lose their loyalty. So he built two alternative sanctuaries, in which he installed altars resting on golden calves: one in Dan, the other in Bethel.

This relieved his political problem but ensured his infamy in the annals of Israel's history. The pro-Davidic author of the books of Kings makes this clear. Without exception, the kings of the north "did evil in the eyes of the Lord." Often the author gets specific by charging some king with "walking in the ways of Jeroboam and in his sin, which he had caused Israel to commit" (1 Kings 15:26).

The period of the divided kingdom was a time of political intrigue, military conflicts and religious apostasy. The Lord finally sent judgment on Israel in the form of the powerful Assyrians. In 722 B.C. Shalmanezer V besieged and destroyed Samaria and deported 27,000 inhabitants of the nation (2 Kings 17:3-6). The ten tribes were assimilated into native populations.

The southern kingdom, called Judah, was a different story, in part. Though the dynasty of David continued, his descendants did not inherit his devotion. The authors of Kings and Chronicles tell us that most "did evil in the eyes of the Lord" by tolerating religious syncretism. Despite the efforts of occasional reformers, such as Hezekiah and Josiah, Judah also provoked the Lord. Judgment came in the form of Nebuchadnezzar, king of Babylon, who razed Jerusalem in 586 B.C.

What happened to God's promise to David that his throne would never end? Had God abandoned his people and his promise? During these years of crisis, prophets appeared in Judah offering an answer to that question. Isaiah, for example, preached that all nations—even the mighty Assyrian empire—were merely tools of God's plan for the final salvation of humankind. Judah's suffering would produce "a remnant of Israel" that would return to their homeland and preside over a coming age of righteousness and peace.

Though the northern kingdom was entirely lost, Judah suffered exile for only seventy years. When Cyrus of Persia conquered Babylon, he allowed the Jews to return and rebuild their city and their temple. This they did under the leadership of Zerubbabel (who rebuilt the temple), Ezra (who brought the people back to the law) and Nehemiah (who rebuilt the walls of Jerusalem). Here, under the prophetic ministries of Haggai, Zechariah and Malachi, the Old Testament concludes.

Intertestamental Times

Though most Bibles simply add the New Testament to the prophecies of the Old, nearly four hundred years of history unfolded between Malachi and Matthew. We may view this period as God's preparation of the world for the coming of the Messiah, Jesus of Nazareth.

At the end of the Old Testament, Judah was a tiny vassal state of the mighty Persian empire. So it remained until in 333 B.C., when Alexander the Great of Macedonia (northern Greece) subdued Persia and assumed authority over the Jews. Upon Alexander's death, his power passed on to four of his generals. The Jews, heirs of ancient Israel, fell under the jurisdiction of Ptolemy, whose state centered in Alexandria, Egypt.

In a sense Alexander's conquests prepared the world for the Christian faith. First, Greek philosophy spread into conquered lands. Greek ideas of monotheism, immortality and morality formed a point of contact between Christianity and the pagan world.

Second, Greek appeared as the common trade language in all the Mediterranean world and remained so for nearly five hundred years. This enabled people like the apostle Paul to preach in a single language over a broad geographical area. During the Ptolemaic period, scholars translated the Old Testament into Greek (the Septuagint) and thus made the Bible available to hosts of new readers.

In 198 B.C. the Seleucids, the Syrian segment of Alexander's empire, annexed Palestine. Within a generation the Syrian king, Antiochus Epiphanes, instituted a policy of oppression against the Jews and outlawed their religion. When soldiers attempted to force Mattathias, the high priest, to sacrifice to pagan gods, he and his family instigated a rebellion. By means of guerrilla warfare, the so-called Maccabean Revolt successfully shed the shackles of the Seleucids and established the free state of Israel.

Freedom, however, was short-lived. The Maccabean rulers fell into the same trap as their forefathers. Corruption helped to guarantee their eventual fall, which came in 63 B.C. at the hands of the Romans. Twenty-three years later the Roman senate passed the scepter to Herod the Great, "King of the Jews," who ruled the land when Jesus was born in Bethlehem.

Jesus of Nazareth
The story of Jesus, his disciples and the early development of Chris-

tianity is recorded in the pages of the New Testament. Two of the Gospels—Matthew and Luke—attribute the birth of Jesus to an act of God. The Lord spoke to a Jewish peasant girl, Mary, and her husband-to-be named Joseph. He told them that by the power of the Holy Spirit she would give birth to a son and they were to name him Yeshua (Jesus), which in Hebrew means "the Lord saves." According to the Gospels, these descendants of David did just as they were told. And God miraculously gave them a son.

Beyond these birth narratives of Matthew and Luke, we know almost nothing about Jesus' early years. When Jesus was nearly thirty, however, his cousin, John, began to preach in the Judean wilderness and baptize in the Jordan River. He told the crowds who went out to hear him that he was a herald for a leader yet to come.

Jesus' own baptism by John proved to be a profound spiritual experience. Immediately afterward, he suffered satanic assaults for forty days in the wilderness, and then launched his three-year mission in Israel. The first year was marked by relative obscurity, the second by popularity and the third by adversity.

During the first year Jesus concentrated on two objectives: reaching out to numbers of people and gathering a small band of disciples: Peter, Matthew, John the son of Zebedee and others. After a few months in the south, Jesus concentrated on the villages of Galilee, away from official Judaism in Jerusalem.

As his reputation spread the second year, he gave himself to wider circles of preaching, teaching and working miracles. The theme of his message was "the gospel of the kingdom." The true kingdom, he said, was the personal reign of God in human lives, and he had come to inaugurate that rule. The arrival of the kingdom was the fulfillment of the Old Testament hope. But in order to "receive," "enter" or "inherit" the kingdom, men and women must repent and believe, humbly accepting its privileges and submitting to its demands like little children.

In teaching his disciples, Jesus explained what it meant to live as people of the kingdom. Perhaps the best example of the new law of the kingdom appears in his Sermon on the Mount. A disciple's righteousness, he said, is unlike the religions of the Pharisees and the pagans. The Jewish leaders called Pharisees practiced a strict faith that often slipped into hypocrisy. In sharp contrast, pagans, who lived without the guidance of the law, used religion as an excuse for selfish gratification. Righteousness, Jesus told his disciples, must spring from a new heart.

Jesus' miracles were themselves a type of teaching. Most of them were healings used as signs of God's kingdom and Jesus' authority. The impact of these "signs and wonders" carried Jesus to the heights of his popularity when he fed five thousand Passover pilgrims. The crowd was so elated that they tried to make Jesus king. Jesus, however, was convinced that the people totally misunderstood his mission. He withdrew quietly to more isolated regions in order to inform his close friends about his true purpose.

Jesus' popularity with the people, however, provoked the Jewish authorities to jealousy and led to the last phase of his public ministry: adversity. Herod Antipas, the ruler of Galilee, feared that Jesus might be the Messiah whom John the Baptist had predicted. So with the help of some of the Pharisees, he laid plans to arrest Jesus and kill him. Jesus learned of the plot, however, and fled to Judea with his disciples.

After several months of preaching, Jesus made his final pilgrimage to Jerusalem for Passover. Accompanied by a large procession, he entered the temple, where he drove out the peddlers of sacrificial animals. On the eve of Passover, Jesus and his twelve disciples celebrated their last meal together. Late that night, soldiers sent by the high priest arrested Jesus.

Before the Sanhedrin, the Jewish high court, Jesus was convicted of blasphemy. Since the Sanhedrin had no authority to execute him, they rushed him to the Roman governor, Pontius Pilate, who sentenced him to death by crucifixion. Soldiers carried out the order: a painful death on a cross.

The Birth of Christianity
Within days rumors were circulating in Jerusalem that Jesus was no

longer dead. He had risen from the grave. The disciples regathered, and two months later, empowered by a new Spirit, they began preaching in Jerusalem's synagogues that Jesus was the promised Messiah; God had confirmed it by raising him from the dead. Forgiveness of sins and the power of the Spirit, they said, were available to anyone who repented and accepted Jesus as Lord.

Among the new believers were some who spoke Greek. They were called Hellenists. Their increasing numbers alarmed the Jewish authorities. One Hellenist leader named Stephen was stoned to death by an angry mob after he dared to challenge Jewish traditions. The instigator of this assault was a Pharisee, Paul of Tarsus. Intent on destroying the new heresy, Paul set out for Damascus. But on the way he had a vivid encounter with the resurrected Jesus—an encounter that transformed him into a zealous Christian.

Through Paul's tireless missionary efforts, Christianity spread from its Jewish roots in Judea into Gentile cities, from Antioch in Syria to the imperial capital, Rome. When he was unable to visit the fledgling churches, Paul wrote letters to encourage or instruct them. In most cities he faced persecution from pagans or from his fellow Jews. Upon his return from a third missionary journey, Jewish leaders secured his imprisonment in Jerusalem. From there Roman authorities moved him to Caesarea, a coastal town, and later to Rome to await trial. He died during Nero's persecution of Christians, but left his mark upon Christianity through the theology strikingly expressed in his letters.

This is the story that ties together the sixty-six books of the Bible and discloses the epochal realities of the Christian faith.

4
THE RANKS OF THE RESISTANCE
THE HUMAN TRAGEDY

During World War II, Japanese military forces rounded up two thousand foreigners on the Chinese mainland and drove them like cattle into an internment camp. Langdon Gilkey, a young American university instructor, was among the businesspeople, missionaries, educators, monks and other Westerners crowded into the former mission compound. In order to survive, these foreign prisoners were forced to set up their own little civilization.

For two and a half years Gilkey watched the tiny society struggle to make life bearable. Initially enthused about his colleagues' ingenuity, Gilkey gradually came to see their underlying greed. He noted how internees tried to annex a few more inches of living space, how they cheated others out of rations allotted to the community and how they refused to share the extra supplies that arrived from the outside world. People, he discovered, supported community decisions only as long as they profited personally. Beyond that they swindled and stole from their fellow prisoners to gain some personal benefit.

Gilkey came to the conclusion that people are not basically interested in the good of their society. They are fundamentally self-centered. When they have something to gain, they will cheat or attack others. This innate selfishness obviously hurt everyone in the internment camp, yet the little society was powerless to deal with it.[1]

What is wrong with men and women? Why do their dreams for a just and prosperous society so often turn to nightmares of violence and greed?

Modern Views of Human Nature

For nearly three centuries Western nations have accepted the Enlightenment dogma that human nature is basically good. Human problems are external. What humanity needs is more public education and democratic institutions. Given these, people will create a better world for themselves and for one another. Every day, in a host of ways, the world is getting better and better.

In the nineteenth century Marxism arose to challenge this optimistic assessment of human nature. Marx taught, and millions around the world soon believed, that the primary human problem is economic exploitation. The rich take advantage of the poor. They treat the poor like animals in order to amass their own riches. But such cruelty always reaches a breaking point. The exploited revolt and overthrow their oppressors. Revolution! That is the need of the masses.

Experience has now raised disturbing questions about the ideals of both democratic liberalism and revolutionary Marxism. Democratic nations often seem ungovernable, and Marxist communism has been widely repudiated in Europe. Something more basic than either ignorance or oppression is wrong with human beings.

People who refuse to take Christianity seriously often insist that Christians "face the facts." But surely G. K. Chesterton was right when he said that human depravity is the one Christian doctrine that can really be proved. In a day of bitter civil wars, family violence, international terrorism and urban crime, who can in all honesty deny that something is dreadfully wrong with human beings?

The Bible's term for the wrong in men and women is *sin.* Novelists and playwrights have used the word so long for illicit sex that it has assumed a magnetic power in the world of entertainment. Movie magnates and advertising executives, aware of this force, have exploited the term for their own benefit.

Modern people are susceptible to this exploitation because they have been told that our Puritan forebears had an unhealthy attitude toward sex. And they want nothing to do with the repressive Puritans. Most people in the Western world today resent someone telling them what is right or wrong. Many of them believe that is what the Puritans did. So as soon as Christians mention "sin," they usually encounter rather stiff resistance to the continuation of the conversation. "Morality is what got the Puritans all messed up."

As a result of this resistance to the Christians' concept of sin and their use of the word, people are dying on every hand of a disease that they refuse to name. They have enlisted in a conspiracy of silence, apparently supposing that elimination of the word means elimination of the condition.

The subject of sin may be unpleasant, but like our doctor's report of our physical exam, it may be necessary if we are ever to regain our health. Before physicians can treat an illness effectively, they have to identify it. Many of us are reluctant to go for a physical examination, but we know that if we are ever going to feel better we have to—as we say—"take our medicine."

In that sense the Christian doctrine of sin is itself very good news. We know what's wrong with us, and the sickness can be treated.

Many doctors in our society do not think so. They are telling people that our human condition is hopeless. They report that our problem is in our genes or our society or the stars; there isn't anything we can do about our condition. We are not responsible. But we are also not curable! That is not very good news.

In contrast to this determinism, the Christian doctrine of sin is good news indeed. Not only does the Christian faith confront the basic human sickness head-on, but it also affirms that men and women were meant for health, for full and fruitful lives. Christianity refuses to accept the sorry human condition as permanent. With the right treatment, the best days are ahead.

The Meaning of Sin

What, then, does a Christian mean by *sin?* Without some understanding of this universal human condition, we are doomed to miss the whole point of the Bible's story and of the Christian faith. Sin lies behind the call of Abraham, the exodus from Egypt, the law at Sinai, the Davidic kingdom, the promise of Messiah and the birth of Jesus Christ. The universality of sin makes the Christian gospel perpetually new.

As Christians use the term, *sin* means two things. First, sin is an act—or, at times, a failure to act. It is either a failure to obey the law of God or some action contrary to the standards of God. This is the way we commonly use the word when we say someone "sinned" or "committed a sin." We usually think of such things as stealing or lying or adultery. And the Bible makes clear that these are sins. But behind the action there is the passion. This too is sin. Murder is the fruit of hatred; hatred is the seed of murder. The two are inextricably united.

One of the most widely read works from the ancient world is Aurelius Augustine's *Confessions,* a kind of autobiography of his soul. At one point he tells about an incident from his childhood. Along with some friends he stole a load of pears from a tree near his home.

"I chose to steal," he said, "not because I was compelled to by poverty or hunger, but just from a bellyful of sin. . . . I didn't take pleasure in what I stole—I just enjoyed stealing and the sinning." He didn't even eat the pears. He threw them at the hogs, just because he knew it was wrong.

That was sin. It was an act, a wrong committed against his neighbor. But it was more. Slowly Augustine came to see that it was also an offense against God.

Christianity stresses that the conception of sin cannot be separated from the idea of God, because sin is not only contrary to the rules of God, it is an offense against God himself. Sin not only attacks the standards of God; it destroys one's relationship with God. The Bible speaks of God as the source of all good. He is the very definition of truth and beauty and goodness. All that he has made is good, and the rules he gave were made to keep it good. So sin is more than an illegal act; it is also a personal affront.

That suggests that sin has another sense. First it is an act; second it is a condition. It is the state of rebellion against God in which we all live. Christians call this condition "original sin" because it is basic to human experience. It is the soil out of which the acts sprout and grow. It is the state of rebellion from which we launch all of our attacks against God's authority.

Christians also call it "original" because it is not just a personal problem. It afflicts all humanity. In his highly acclaimed *Gulag Archipelago* Aleksandr Solzhenitsyn says, "If only there were evil people somewhere insidiously committing evil deeds, and it were necessary only to separate them from the rest of us and destroy them. But the line dividing good and evil cuts through the heart of every human being. And who is willing to destroy a piece of his own heart?"[2]

Perhaps the most profound analysis of sin in all literature is found in the first book of the Bible. The Genesis story of Adam and Eve tells how God placed the two of them in the Garden of Eden to work and care for it. He allowed them to eat of any tree in the garden, with a single exception: they could not eat of the tree of the knowledge of good and evil.

In time, however, the crafty tempter came to Eve and asked, "Did God really say, 'You must not eat from any tree in the garden'?" His first move was to plant the seed of doubt by questioning God's word.

So the woman followed his lead. She answered, "We may eat fruit from the trees in the garden, but God did say, 'You must not eat fruit from the tree that is in the middle of the garden, and you must not touch it, or you will die.' " Her added prohibition about touching the tree indicates that she had already begun to distrust God's goodness.

"You will not surely die," the serpent said to her. "For God knows that when you eat of it your eyes will be opened, and you will be like

God, knowing good and evil" (Gen 3:1-5). That was an effective move. He appealed to her pride. He suggested that she reach beyond her assigned lot in life.

So she questioned her God-given life and followed her vanity: she seized the fruit and ate it. Then she gave some to Adam and he ate. The eyes of both of them were suddenly opened. They both knew that they were naked and unprepared to face God. So they sewed fig leaves together in a futile attempt to cover their shame. But when they heard God walking in the garden, they hid from him.

Their act of sin led to their condition of sin. Rejection of God's law and their mad pursuit of something better resulted in their estrangement from God. So the Lord God banished them from the Garden of Eden.

This loss of paradise is the Bible's way of describing "original sin." It is the condition in which all people find themselves, separated from God yet longing for the inner contentment they once knew in his presence. We are like marionettes that have cut their own strings in the hope of finding another way to dance, but find out too late that without the strings they cannot dance at all.

The Consequences of Sin

As a consequence of human sinfulness we all experience a sort of gravitational pull toward self-centeredness. It is much easier, as Langdon Gilkey discovered, to do the selfish deed, and to keep on doing it, than to do the generous and neighborly thing. Sinning is like skiing. The ease and excitement are on the way down the mountain. The trick is getting back up to the top. Most of us know that to get to the top we really need outside help.

Unfortunately, human help in overcoming this gravitational pull is limited. Most societies recognize the problem and try to restrict its damaging effects. They pass laws and create police forces and build prisons, but no society—so far as I am aware—has ever overcome the downward drag. So the security of life and property remains one of the fundamental responsibilities of any government.

This human propensity also explains why sins are so habit-forming. The first exciting experience of a sin makes the second easier. The second encourages the third, and so on, until we find that we do not want to think of life without the fleeting pleasure of the sin. We reach a point where we cannot give it up. We are hooked.

By that time it should be obvious that we cannot have the pleasure of sin without paying a price. Something dies in us when we insist on recapturing the delight of the forbidden fruit. We surrender a bit more freedom to the habit. We stoop a bit closer to the bestial level. Lower and lower we go until human freedom of choice is gone.

Sin, then, is a form of slow death. "A man reaps what he sows," said the apostle Paul. "The one who sows to please his sinful nature, from that nature will reap destruction" (Gal 6:7-8). A child disobediently plays with matches and gets burned. A man abuses alcohol and gradually destroys his mind and his marriage. A woman cheats on her husband and loses her children, her home and ultimately even her lover.

Since the 1970s we've heard a great deal about a strange American disease called anorexia. It afflicts people in a mysterious way. They do not want food. They literally starve themselves to death, some of them in the belief that they will look better and feel better if they do not eat. Sin is a disease that works in a similar way. It convinces us that we will be happier and more admired by others if we will only refuse the food that might mean our health.

The ultimate consequence of sin, then, is death. The two are inseparably linked. "The statistics on death," British playwright George Bernard Shaw once said, "are quite impressive." The reason, says Christianity, lies in the nature of death. It is more than a biological fact. It is a consequence of sin.

If this poisonous fruit is ever to be uprooted, we will have to consider drastic measures. Our lives are fields that primarily contain weeds. We cannot produce strawberries. We can mow the weeds, but that effort alone will never produce acceptable fruit. If we want that fruit we will have to go deeper. We must plow the whole field and start again with new plants.

The Christian view of sin is realistic because it explains both the dignity of men and women as creatures of God and the ruin of people in their self-chosen rebellion. Men and women have joined the ranks of the resistance. They are wandering through life far from their spiritual home, the only source of their true identity. Above every other concern, then, they need to find their way back to their Father's house.

5
SPEAKING TERMS
FAITH

Robert Louis Stevenson, the well-known poet and novelist, grew up in a home that confessed faith in God. As an adult, however, Stevenson lapsed into agnosticism. Only as he lay dying in faraway Samoa did he rediscover the faith of his childhood. Rheumatic and speechless—only forty-four years old—Stevenson held a note pad on his knees. On this he scratched simple messages for those attending him. Shortly before he died, he reached for the pad and scrawled: "Stately music; enter God."[1]

Christians have always insisted that faith is essential. People cannot possibly find fulfillment as long as they resist God. To find life and spiritual health they must look to the Hidden World.

"Thou hast made us for thyself," Augustine, the influential bishop in fifth-century North Africa, once prayed. "And our hearts are restless until they find their rest in thee."

If birds are made for the air, human beings are made for life with God. You can thrust a bird under water and it will die. It is out of its element. It was not made for water; it was designed for air. Just so, when people try to survive without faith, they experience a slow death.

This faith, however, is no longer a self-evident term. In our secular times we need to ask, What is the Christian faith? What are the distinctive Christian beliefs, and what difference do they make if we accept them?

The Meaning of Faith

It is necessary to press the meaning of faith because so many people in our society assume that faith is a kind of psychological key we use to open doors into an inner world of comfort and confidence. These people encourage the mystical moods of the soul, convinced that in them they can find true peace and freedom from stress. In all this their eyes are turned inward, in the firm assurance that true religion is found in an attitude of the soul. They call it "faith."

Before we can seriously consider the Christian faith, we have to confront this widespread line of thinking and make clear that Christianity is not another path to "peace of mind" or "spiritual health." The men and women of faith we meet in the Bible are never introspective mystics, trying to work themselves into a mood of faith. On the contrary, they look away from themselves to the works of God in creation and history.

In Scripture, faith always rests on the good news of God's actions in our space-time world. When Jesus urged men and women to "have faith in God," he never spoke of it as some mysterious power that normal people would find incredible. Faith, as the Bible uses the term, is an attitude toward life that is available to all people. It is not something that strangely religious people pump up out of the deep recesses of their souls. It is a decision that all people make when they are confronted with a convincing testimony of God's action in time.

When the Bible speaks of faith, then, it usually intends either of two related ideas. One is faith as beliefs. It stands for Christianity's description of reality. It appeals to a series of events that created certain fundamental convictions about God and man and Christ and salvation. These beliefs are basic to Christianity; they help to form and sustain that community of faith we call the church.

The other idea of faith, as the Bible uses the word, is trust. This idea goes beyond the rational element in Christian beliefs and emphasizes the relational element of faith. In this sense faith is akin to commitment, risk and faithfulness—qualities of a special relationship between two people. It is what the Bible means by "knowing" someone.

These two meanings of faith are often intertwined in the Bible because the purpose of the truths *about* God is to lead men and women to personal trust *in* God.

It might help to think of the Christian faith as a letter. Imagine a young woman, living with her family, who exchanges letters with a boyfriend living across the country. In one of these letters, the young man proposes marriage.

When the mail carrier delivers the proposal, he or she is part of an event of immense importance. The event bears a message. When the daughter in the family reads the letter she understands the significance of the event, and she faces a major decision. Will she marry the young man or refuse him?

If she says yes in her heart, she will have to tell her family. When she does, other family members are drawn into the relationship and immediately begin to discuss among themselves the meaning of the wedding and their part in the new family.

In a similar way, the basis of the Christian faith is first an *event* of immense importance. God sends his message to humankind and wraps it in an event: "God was in Christ, reconciling the world unto himself" (2 Cor 5:19 KJV).

Second, the basis of faith appears as *gospel.* The witnesses of the event share what they have seen and heard. That is the good news that we call the gospel. When men and women hear this story they either believe it or reject it. The telling of the story, like the proposal in the letter, calls for a personal response.

Faith is a yes. It reflects a person's *trust* in the One who sent the message. Then, finally, faith appears as explanation and application within the family. As the church reflects upon the meaning of the gospel, faith assumes the form of *beliefs* and creeds.

The event and the story, then, are always fundamental to the Christian faith. Human feelings and moods are never primary. God comes first. Faith is always response to God's initiative in Christ.

Some people find this particularity of the gospel offensive. Why can't all people everywhere have direct access to the truth? Christians see no value in arguing possibilities; they insist that wisdom deals with actualities. The offense of the gospel's historicity must remain.

And yet this historicity has a hidden value. It means the Word of God—event and gospel—is accessible to all who will listen to the story. Children may not grasp instructions. Stubborn people may not follow advice. Weak people may be unable to obey rules. But everyone can listen to a story. And those who listen may believe.

People are so prone to turn the gospel into something other than the good news from God that we must stress its uniqueness. It is not some sort of *Poor Richard's Almanac* offering advice on rearing children, making money and serving God. It is not a short course on ethics, updating the Ten Commandments for moderns. It is not even a religious tract, prescribing five easy steps to God.

The gospel is first, last and always good news about how God came to humanity and made his move for peace. It is an event that belonged on the front pages of the Jerusalem newspapers in the spring of A.D. 30. It is an event, a story, a bit of history.

Faith as Trust

The gospel story, like the proposal in the letter, calls for a response. We will never understand the Christian faith if we try to examine it from a safe distance. It is not a frog's leg to dissect and classify.

Truth, as Jesus used the term, is a personal reality. A person who wants to settle all the questions in his or her mind before deciding for or against the Christian faith is headed up a blind alley. This person is adopting an attitude that makes it impossible to see straight while looking at the Christian faith.

Some people refuse to take the gospel seriously because they try to judge Christianity by the standards of science. But that is foolhardy. Truth in a laboratory is determined by testing, again and again, under controlled conditions so that the experiment will yield the same results time after time. But Christianity—like art and love and history—will not surrender to those standards. The Christian faith is not and never will be scientific in that sense of the word.

The gospel is the story of a unique event; there is no way to replay it. Nor is God an object like other objects. What would he look like under a microscope? The scientific method is not designed to render a judgment on Christianity.

Some people find that fact unacceptable. The successes of science have generated an unbecoming arrogance in some people. But that doesn't change the fact that science samples only a small slice of reality. What scientific instrument do we use to plumb the depths of Bach's musical genius or measure the mystery of a mother's love for her infant?

While Christianity cannot be tested by scientific methods, it is not, as a consequence, mere superstition. As one apostle put it, "We have not followed cunningly devised fables" (2 Pet 1:16 KJV). The gospel is good news. It is divine truth revealed in events that really happened. Christianity does not rest on myths. It welcomes inquiry. It is prepared to present evidence and state cases.

It is important to make that point in a day of competing claims and widespread gullibility. Many people really do believe the old adage "It doesn't matter what you believe as long as you're sincere." But anyone who will take time for second thoughts will realize that sincerely held convictions can be dead wrong.

Most Christians empathize with G. K. Chesterton when he says, "What we suffer from to-day is humility in the wrong place. Modesty has moved from the organ of ambition. Modesty has settled upon the organ of conviction; where it was never meant to be. A man was meant to be doubtful about himself, but undoubting about the truth; this has been exactly reversed."[2]

At the same time Christians ought not to overstate their case. They must hold fast to all that God has revealed, but they know that when they attempt to speak of God they are on the threshold of infinity and eternity.

In one of his last messages to the children of Israel, Moses said, "The secret things belong to the LORD our God, but the things revealed belong to us and to our children forever, that we may follow all the words of this law" (Deut 29:29). One of the most difficult assignments in setting forth the Christian faith is sorting out the secret things from the revealed things.

The Christian faith rests upon adequate, *not* overwhelming, evidence. It is evidence to induce trust, not to settle lawsuits. An effective presentation of the gospel will always respect the freedom of the hearer, simply because true faith must be personal faith. Everyone who enters the kingdom does so freely. That is the condition of any personal relationship. God is not interested in slaves within the kingdom; he wants children. That means genuine faith will always include choice, love and commitment, realities of life that cannot be coerced.

The Language of Faith
In stating their beliefs, however, Christians face a major problem. They are confessing realities that are beyond normal human experiences. God is eternal, infinite and invisible. How can human languages hope to convey meaning from realms beyond our five senses? And yet we have no other language. When we say God is a Father or a King or a Shepherd, we are using terms from human experience, and these cannot possibly be accepted at face value.

The oldest, and perhaps the best, explanation of Christian language is the way of analogy. This rests upon the fact that God is the Creator of the universe and human beings are his creatures. So there is a fundamental relationship between God and people. The Bible points to this relationship when it says, "God created man *in his own image*"—as a kind of imperfect mirror of God's own character. Such a likeness between two people or two things we call *analogy*.

The language of analogy, then, expresses partial—not complete—similarity between two people or things. In speaking of God we use terms that carry only a limited correspondence of meaning. When we say, for example, "Mr. Simpson is certainly healthy," and a bit later, "Sun Valley is healthy," we mean Mr. Simpson is genuinely healthy. His blood pressure is normal. He has no infection. He is not overweight. We mean Sun Valley is conducive to health. It has fresh air and lots of sunshine. It is healthy in a derivative sense.

In a similar way, when we say "God is powerful" and "Stalin was powerful," we mean God is omnipotent. He possesses power in its fullness. Stalin was powerful only in a derivative sense. Millions of people submitted to his authority, but he did not have power in and of himself.

The language of the faith, then, is not the language of science or any other modern field of knowledge. It is the language of common people—more than adequate to lead us to the truth.

What makes the faith distinctively Christian? How can we sort out the genuine item from the thousands of substitutes and counterfeits in today's religious market? Are there, as a consequence of the revelation of God in Christ, special marks of the Christian faith? The bewildering variety of contemporary religious claims seems to argue against the possibility. Pluralism seems to be the order of the day. How can anyone speak of "*the* faith"?

That is not an easy question to answer. Through two thousand years Christians have expressed their faith in a host of forms and styles. Believers probably always will disagree on the best way to state their convictions. Is "total depravity," for example, an item of "the faith"? What about "eternal security"? Christianity is a historical movement, and determining the precise borders of any historical movement is a persistent problem. In many areas a believer should not pretend to speak for God.

When an antique hunter is in search of an heirloom, he or she has in mind the hallmarks of the original. In our quest for the Christian faith, it might be helpful to list the hallmarks.

The Marks of Faith

The first hallmark of the Christian faith is Jesus Christ. What is God like? Look at Jesus Christ. What is human nature like? Check with Jesus Christ. What is God doing in the world? Consider Jesus Christ.

A total stranger to Christianity may find this focus on one person a little surprising. After all, Muhammad taught submission to Allah. And Buddha pointed to Nirvana, the ultimate. Most founders of religions deliver to their followers some great truths. But in Christianity, Jesus is more than a teacher; he is the truth.

Christianity makes no sense apart from Jesus Christ. Faith in him sets Christianity off from the other major theistic faiths, Judaism and Islam. Christians have always considered him more than an influential rabbi or a prophet of God.

Jesus made unique, exclusive claims about his relationship to God. "I am the bread of life," he said (Jn 6:35). And Christianity arose when men and women found it impossible to deny his claims. They faced the startling possibilities of his assertions, and found that worship was the only appropriate response.

Worship of someone who appears to be human raises additional problems that we will have to face in time, but for now let this fact serve as a guide to the meaning of Christian faith: it concentrates on Jesus Christ.

The second hallmark of the Christian faith is the Bible. Almost all we know about Jesus Christ—his background in Judaism, his message to his contemporaries, his death at the hands of the Romans, the reports of his resurrection—comes from the Bible. The Old Testament creates the concepts of the Christian faith—creation, redemption, covenant, kingdom, Messiah—and the New Testament sets forth the center and climax of this faith: the Word, God's message, in flesh.

The Bible is something like a charter for the Christian faith. Like other movements, the church expanded into new times and new cultures. This growth meant adaptation to new languages and new patterns of thought. Under these conditions an institution can easily wander far from the purpose and intention of its founder. Christianity, however, continued to look to the Scriptures as the standard for faith. As a result the church, from time to time, has discovered its errors and returned to its original mission.

The third hallmark for identifying the Christian faith is the teaching of the church. The gospel creates a community of faith. Christians do not survive in lonely isolation; faith is followed by baptism into this community of believers. And this fellowship of faith helps believers grow and guards them from errors and excesses in their personal faith.

There is no other way. It might be tempting to try spinning out a new version of the faith from one's own private impressions of the Bible. This, in fact, is done. But the term for that is not *Christianity* but *cult*. The fact is, anyone who claims to be presenting the Christian faith must constantly reckon with the witness of the church throughout the world and across the centuries.

In a rootless age, Christians must resist the temptation to reject tradition out of hand. The continuing existence of the Christian church and the creeds it has written over the centuries testify to the strength of that supranational community and the faith that sustains it.

Through the Christian centuries, the churches wrote creeds and confessions in order to nurture the weak in faith and to guard the zealous from error. These statements of faith provide some balance for believers. They give contemporary Christians perspective and help them sort out essential doctrines from faddish extremes.

The final hallmark of the Christian faith is what I like to call "good sense." Some people may prefer to call it "reason" in the sense of "reasonable." The label isn't as important as the thought. By "good sense" I mean the conviction every Christian has that the gospel "fits" reality as he or she has experienced it. The Word of God "fits" life as we have come to know it. It is appropriate.

This "good sense" is not the way people usually think. As we have seen, common opinions are often at odds with God's truth. Our human thoughts are often not God's thoughts. The gospel often strikes a person as sheer foolishness. And yet there is another side to the matter.

Think of the story Jesus told about the son who demanded his inheritance from his father and left home for a distant country. He spent all his money, and while feeding pigs he suddenly had second thoughts about life back home (Lk 15:11-17). The story simply says, "when he came to his senses." Now what does that mean? In the experience of faith most Christians recognize a moment or a time of reflection when they come to see how the gospel makes sense to them. The Christian explanation of life and reality fits their own perceptions of reality.

Our perceptions do change. They are shaped by assumptions about reality that we absorb from our families, our acquaintances and our culture. It seems, therefore, that the Christian faith must always be contemporary. It may challenge our assumptions or it may confirm our assumptions, but it cannot fail to engage them. Otherwise the gospel would never translate into faith. It would strike us as fantasy or nonsense, never the truth.

In his book *Mere Christianity* C. S. Lewis shows that men and women often surrender their convictions, or as we say "lose their faith," not because they are convinced by new evidence that their beliefs are fallacious, but because their emotions or imaginations overwhelm them.

Take, for example, a boy learning to swim. His reason tells him that an unsupported human body can remain afloat in water. He has seen dozens of people float and swim. But the whole question is whether he can go on believing this truth when the instructor leads him into the water and it is "sink or swim." Will he suddenly cease to believe it, and listen to the voice of panic and go under?

The same thing happens with Christians. They confront the faith and accept it as a reasonable account of reality. But what happens? Within a few weeks they run into trouble or meet people who ridicule their Christian commitment, and all of a sudden, says Lewis, their emotions "rise up and carry out a sort of blitz" on their beliefs. This rebellion of our moods is the test of our faith.[3]

If we questioned a hundred people who had lost their faith in Christianity, how many of them would you suppose turned away from the faith because someone reasoned them out of it? Don't most simply drift away?

Style, events, public opinions and other social conditions play upon our minds and choices—and often lead us astray. This assault on faith points up the need for what Lewis calls "training the habit of faith." Christians must hold the great doctrines of Christianity before their minds daily. That is the purpose of the disciplines of daily prayer, Bible reading and churchgoing. Faith needs a constant reminder. It will not remain alive in the mind unless we feed it regularly.

6
THE ULTIMATE RULER
GOD ABOVE US

Some years ago a manufacturer of children's clothing ran an advertisement in *The New York Times Magazine* inviting children to draw "what God looks like to you." More than 1,700 drawings were sent in. One of them, by a five-year-old, had two clouds. The caption read: "This is Mr. and Mrs. God. They look like clouds. They are very old."

Most of us, I suspect, tend to rely on rather foggy images of God. People on the streets of Western nations today think of God much as a sailor thinks of the ship's lifeboat. The sailor knows the lifeboat is there but hopes there will never be an occasion to use it.

That is not the faith that the Bible describes, because it is not the God that the Bible discloses.

The first article of the Apostles' Creed, used in many Christian churches every Sunday, says, "I believe in God the Father Almighty, Maker of heaven and earth." But what is God like?

The Attributes of God
The words and phrases that Christians use to portray God are called

attributes. The term simply stands for the characteristics of a person. President Harry Truman, for example, was blunt. President Abraham Lincoln was courageous. Some attributes of people are positive and some are negative. Most of us appreciate the positive ones such as kindness and understanding, but we dislike brusqueness and greed.

When Christians speak of God as the Bible describes him, they must hold in constant tension two fundamental convictions about him.

First, God is unlike us. He is, as we say, "beyond" us. He is not a human being, and human beings are not God. An unbridgeable gulf separates the Creator from his creatures. He is infinite and holy. We, men and women, are finite and sinful. Theologians call this distinctiveness of God *transcendence,* meaning he is "other" than we are.

Second, God is like us. He formed the universe and then created man and woman in his own "image," capable of communion with him. As a consequence, human beings have the potential to know God and to share his purposes on earth. This created kinship is a reflection of what theologians call God's *immanence.* Somehow he is present in this world that he has made.

Jeremiah, the ancient Hebrew prophet, linked these two basic truths about God in one of his messages to his people:

"Am I only a God nearby," declares the LORD,
"and not a God far away?
Can anyone hide in secret places
so that I cannot see him?" declares the LORD.
"Do not I fill heaven and earth?" declares the LORD.
(Jer 23:23-24)

When Christians describe this "faraway" and "nearby" deity, they rely on these two basic convictions. Since God is unlike human beings, we have to speak in negative terms. We say that God is invisible when we mean he is not visible, or we say he is immutable, meaning not changeable, or infinite, meaning not finite, or incomprehensible, meaning not comprehensible. In this approach we try to describe God by removing from him the limitations of human existence. We call this the "negative way" to God.

At the same time, since God is also like humankind, Christians speak of God in positive terms. They say that God is almighty, perfectly good, omnipresent and perfectly wise. In this approach to the attributes of God, we take some human virtue and raise it to eminence—that is, to the highest degree. So we call this "the way of eminence."

Thoughtful Christians have always confessed that every description of God is woefully inadequate. Attempting to describe God is like trying to picture a deepening Arizona sunset or a gliding gull over San Francisco Bay. Human language is simply incapable of depicting much of reality.

Still, Christians cannot remain silent. People who refuse to speak at all of the God beyond us go too far. He is veiled in mystery. That is true. But he has revealed himself. That is also true. He has spoken through the gardenia's fragrance and the galaxy's rhythm. But he has disclosed himself supremely through Jesus Christ. We cannot act as though nothing had happened. The fact that we cannot describe God fully does not consign us to silence. We have genuine, though not exhaustive, knowledge of God.

Let us speak, then, of this God who has revealed himself to us. In this chapter let's think of the God who is "far away," and in the next chapter we'll ponder this same God who is "near."

God the Creator

In the Bible God comes first. Genesis 1:1 says, "In the beginning God . . ." These are the Bible's opening words. Nothing comes before him. But the God who is there—before all things—chooses to create. That is basic to the Christian view of God. The personal God of eternity freely chose to bring worlds into being. Nothing except God exists on its own. Not nature. Not humanity. Only God stands in self-sufficient splendor. The Christian faith, then, recognizes two fundamental categories of reality: God, the self-existent One, and the visible and invisible creation—the dependent universe.

If that distinction seems to make much ado about very little, appearances are deceiving. We may be forgetting that millions of people in the world today, as we have seen, hold to pantheism, a faith that equates God with the universe. It teaches that the natural world is the self-unfolding of God. In this view God is depersonalized; he is the name we give to nature, the life force that surges through all that exists. He is not personal; he never talks; he hears no prayers. He is *It.*

In Christianity, however, the Creator stands in sovereign and self-sufficient majesty apart from the natural order. He made it, and he sustains it, but he is not it. The Westminster Confession of Faith, written in 1646, speaks for most Christians when it says God has "all life, glory, goodness and blessedness in himself." He alone is all-sufficient. He has no need of any creature he has made.

In one of his books J. S. Whale tells a story about a youngster who was too restless to get to sleep one warm summer evening. He climbed out of his bed, crossed the room to the window, peeped through a chink in the blind and saw his mother on the lawn, playing croquet with some strange people. Naturally, she was entirely unoccupied with him, and it came to his little mind as a shock. He had always assumed that she existed for him and was, as it were, adjectival to him rather than a being who enjoyed an identity of her own. He now learned that she had a life of her own.[1]

In a similar way, God has a life of his own. Christian thought has always confessed this mystery of God's self-existence. It is basic to faith in the Creator.

The Christian also has to add a balancing truth. The Bible never considers creation merely a once-for-all event; it is also a continuous process. The God who brings galaxies and giraffes and goldfish into existence is also the Lord who sustains them. He is behind or within all physical processes, all reproductive powers, all harmonies and systems of nature.

In their indictment of Israel for unfaithfulness to the covenant with God, the Hebrew prophets time and again identify the Lord of the covenant with this omnipotent God of creation. "He who forms the mountains," Amos cries, "and creates the wind . . . He who made the Pleiades and Orion, and turns deep darkness into the morning . . . who calls for the waters of the sea, and pours them out upon the surface of the earth—the LORD is his name" (Amos 4:13; 5:8; 9:6 RSV). The basis of faith in the Lord's steadfast purpose in Israel's history is his faithful presence in creation.

For the Christian, then, as for the prophets, *natural* never means "self-explanatory" but the stable, regular workings of the universe maintained by God. This explains the Christian rejection of deism, which professes faith in a Creator but finds no evidence of his maintenance of creation.

Christian believers have never been happy with Alexander Pope's maxim "the first Almighty Cause / acts not by partial, but by general laws." Christians deny that the vision of the First Cause and his "grand design" in nature is superior to the biblical portrait of the living God of Abraham, Isaac and Jacob. Pope's Almighty Cause is unwilling or unable to administer the universe he has made. So there is no hope for answers to prayers or miracles of deliverance. Human beings are all alone in the universe. Are we to believe, then, that the deist's architect of nature is superior to the Lord of Hosts?

Creation and Science

If we accept the Christian view of creation, are we not left without a rationale for science? Isn't the choice today either science or superstition? So many would have us believe. They recall the centuries-old warfare between science and Scripture— and they do have a point. Science has forced Christians to change many of their ideas about God and the Bible. We now know, for example, that the earth is much older than our ancestors once believed.

But it is also an established fact that modern science arose in Christian lands dominated by faith in a faithful God of creation. Many of the pioneers of modern science were devout Christians. There is no inherent reason that cannot be true today. This is God's world, and Christians should be among the first to understand and appreciate its mysteries.

Since the seventeenth century, Christians have had to assume the role of resistance fighters because so many modern men and women have had an unthinking confidence in science. They have made it the Ultimate Ruler and worshiped at its shrine.

Today we see the dangers of science much more clearly than many did in an earlier age. We now know that it is not the whole of human existence. There are, in fact, threats to human survival on planet earth where science and technology have been applied without thoughtful consideration of purpose. Nuclear warfare and environmental pollution are only two of these dangers. Science, we now know, is far from the messiah we once envisioned. It is now clear that if science does not serve humane purposes rather than destructive ones, the human race is in imminent danger.

In contrast to this implicit faith in the wonders of modern science, the Christian considers the universe a workshop of the will of God. According to Genesis, God saw that creation was good. It conformed to his intention. The Bible, then, does not describe the "how" of creation so much as the "why."

The Scriptures have a special way of stressing the dependence of creation upon the will of God: "By faith we understand that the universe was formed at God's command, so that what is seen was not made out of what was visible" (Heb 11:3). Worlds came into being by the Word of God. The visible world is a product of powers from the Hidden World. God spoke and there was light. God lifted his voice and stars filled the heavens.

This Christian faith in the Maker of heaven and earth is unique, in the ancient world as well as in the modern one. It avoids both polytheism and naturalism.

We know that the ancient Sumerian civilization in Mesopotamia (about 3000 B.C.) held to a mythological polytheism. In the Sumerian creation stories, the sea, the earth and the deep appear as divinities—Nammu, Nin-mah and Enki—engaged in a struggle to bring forth the created world. These myths, recited at great religious festivals, were repeated for purposes of magic. Their power was in the word itself.

The biblical story of creation, which may have borrowed some of the imagery of these myths, is sharply different in its message: Nothing exists apart from God. The word of God appears, but the recitation and incantations are gone. Instead, Genesis affirms that the Lord of the universe creates and sustains all things by the word of God, by his self-revealing Power. Thus the regularity of the natural order—the presupposition of all natural science—is guaranteed by the God who speaks, and whose word is power.

The Purpose of Creation

This description of creation cuts two ways. It not only challenges the polytheism of ancient Sumer but also refutes the naturalism of our own times. The modern idea of nature, with its accidental causes, is an impersonal universe. It knows only a dehumanized creation. Not so in Genesis. The biblical perspective is that behind all reality is the personal, transcendent God. The visible world is the effect of the word of God. It is the expression of a purpose in the Hidden World. So according to the Bible, creation is purposeful. It offers us an answer to "why?" Let me illustrate.

We live in a mile-high city. During the winter months we see our share of snow. When the snows start to fall, my wife puts an assortment of seeds in the bird feeder hanging under the apple tree near the house. The sparrows are there in no time. The starlings and red-winged blackbirds take a bit longer. The magpies, however, are reluctant to venture so close to the house.

I have often wondered, "Why should the big birds be so timid?" I finally got the courage to ask my wife, who is more a student of feathered creatures than I. She explained, "The sparrows are so much quicker than the magpies. They will come closer to the house for their food because they can zip away at the first sound of danger. The magpies are at a great disadvantage. It takes them forever to take off. They are like jumbo jets."

It seemed to make sense. Birds, I take it, do have what we call *instinct*. In other words, behind their behavior is a purpose.

Naturalism gives us no answer to "why?" Its only alternative to a purposeful Creator is time and chance. It cannot explain to us why there should be anything at all.

Some years ago many people in the Western world held that evolution could explain everything. The universe, they said, developed by accident—all that nature needed was time. Given millions of years, this world of apparent design pieced itself together.

You can often detect the absurdity of a position by translating it into cruder terms. Take a human parallel. One day the earth shook and trembled. Rocks flew in all directions. Some of them were piled high along the eastern seaboard of what is now the United States. Over the millennia, winds blew and rains fell. Slowly the sun dried the mud until what we call the Jefferson Monument appeared just as it stands today. No human design was necessary, just forces of nature and time.

If you hold that mindless evolution accounts for the world we live in, that is how you think! Evolutionary science as an explanation of how the natural world operates is illuminating. But evolutionary thinking as an explanation of what the world is all about is nonsense. The absurdity of this line of thinking was highlighted by biologist Edwin Conklin when he said: "The probability of life originating from an accident is comparable to the probability of an unabridged dictionary resulting from an explosion in a printing shop."[2]

Christianity has always insisted that the supreme purpose of creation was man, the sole creature capable of communion with God. The Genesis story reaches its climax in God's breathing life into human flesh. Only Adam and Eve bear the image of God. Creation, then, must serve humane purposes. But men and women, the pinnacle of creation, must serve the purposes of God.

Hymn writer Robert Robinson asked:

Mighty God, while angels bless Thee,
May a mortal lisp Thy Name?
Lord of men, as well as angels,
Thou art every creature's theme.
Lord of every land and nation,

Ancient of eternal days,
Sounded through the wide creation
Be Thy just and endless praise.

Mighty God, While Angels Bless Thee

The Christian doctrine of creation, then, is more than a notion that God probably exists and has brought all things into existence. As the Bible speaks of creation, it often aims at the human will in order to drive men and women to the mercy of God. That is significant because today's society is filled with people who are ready to admit that God exists, but who have never felt the slightest impulse to bow in humble worship of him.

Martin Luther, who had a unique insight into the intention of Scripture, asked in his Small Catechism what it means to believe in God the Father Almighty, Maker of heaven and earth. His answer: "I believe that God has created me and all that exists; that he provides me daily and abundantly with all the necessities of life, protects me from all danger, and preserves me from evil. For all of this I am bound to thank, praise, serve, and obey him."

This is most certainly true. When you turn from the clouds to the Bible, you find that God is more than an old, old man. God the Creator is also more than the invisible Explanation of the ordered universe. He is the majestic Source of life itself, and the awesome personal God before whom we must bow in grateful adoration. He does not ask for our reluctant acknowledgment of his power in nature. He has something far more radical in mind.

1
WHAT IS GOD LIKE?
GOD WITH US

World War II was almost over. News of the armistice had reached the troops, but the actual order to cease fire was still on the way to the front. Then a bursting shell tore open a soldier's flesh. As the blood flowed out of the fatal wound, he said, "Isn't this just like God?"[1]

Everyone, it seems, has some concept of what God is like. Most human beings resist the thought of living in a world that is totally capricious. But what is the real Lord of all like? Are we left to our own personal impressions? Or is there some sure source that we can all trust for an answer?

As we have seen, the Christian Scriptures reveal two important truths about God. In one sense, he is unlike us. He is above us, transcendent in his creative power and majestic holiness. In another sense, he is like us. But how? What can the Almighty Creator possibly have in common with weak and egocentric human beings?

God, like a man or a woman, is personal. By that we mean that he is on the side of persons rather than on the side of things. He is a "he"—a person—not an "it." He is aware of his existence. He thinks and decides and loves. As a person he can relate to us and we to him. That is important.

During the summer months, children are constantly getting lost in the Rocky Mountains near our home. A party of sightseers may be enjoying the scenes of towering pines, cascading waterfalls, drifting white clouds and blue skies. But when someone shouts, "Nicki's gone!" the enjoyment of the crowd vanishes, and concern for the lost child sends people in all directions calling anxiously, "Nicki! Nicki!"

Why this sudden change of mood? Normal human beings recognize that one curly-haired child is more precious to parents and friends than a whole range of vast and towering mountains. A little girl can laugh and speak and pray and love, but mountains can do none of these things.

I am not suggesting that this distinction between persons and things is always easy to recognize. It seems to come with maturity. When they were young, our children, like children everywhere, talked to their teddy bears. The soft little animals were a part of their world. But imperceptibly, the years brought the children to that time in life when they no longer confused their stuffed toys with family members.

If we applied this insight to the life of faith, we would see how childish it is to treat God like a toy. A toy can only fulfill our imaginings. By the power of imagination it becomes what we want. We project our dreams and impose them upon the unsuspecting teddy. But children, in time, learn that brothers and sisters have minds of their own. Persons always do. And God does.

Some people find the thought of a personal God inferior to a concept of a God beyond personality. They refer to God as "the Absolute," "the Ground of Being" or "the Power of the Universe." This is the language of philosophy, however, not faith. Abstractions like "the Absolute" are impersonal, more like powerful forces such as gravity and electricity. How does one trust in force, or love a universal law? Ordinary people find no personal fulfillment in abstract concepts. Only a personal God can deepen friendship and love and commitment within us.

Blaise Pascal, who lived during the era of the French Enlighten-ment, knew well the arguments for and against the existence of God. He once wrote, "The God of the Christians is not a God who is simply the theory of geometric truths. This is the God of the pagans. . . . The God of the Christians is a God of love and consecration, a God who makes them feel their utter misery and his infinite mercy. . . . He makes the soul feel that its peace lies wholly in him, and that it has no joy save to love him."[2]

Once we accept the idea that God is personal, that he is like us in this important sense, then we must face the implications of that fact. It means we must surrender all of our attempts to project our dreams upon God. He is no teddy bear. We can't coax him or cajole him or control him by our prayers or our actions. We never *earn* the friend-ship of another human being, and we do not earn the favor of God.

This personal relationship with God works the other way, too. We must realize that he wants to communicate with us, not control us or use us. He is not interested in overwhelming us; he will not compel our loyalty. He wants us to trust him and love him—freely.

If God is personal, then the deepest meaning of our lives lies not in abstractions and generalities, but in his personal purpose for them. What is it that he wants of us? There is no more significant question in all of life. If God has a purpose for us, that is the final meaning for living.

The Presence of God

This living, personal God is with us in two fundamental ways: He is with us as the Creator, the providential Ruler of the universe, sustain-ing our life from day to day. And he is with us as Savior, inviting us to consider our spiritual rebellion and to receive the offer of forgive-ness extended to us in the gospel of Jesus Christ.

In the first case, God surrounds us with his presence; he envelopes us in his creative life. He is our most basic environment. Just as the sea surrounds and sustains the tuna, or the air envelops and supports the eagle in flight, so God is in the world he has made. He is over us and around us and within us. "In him we live and move and have our being" (Acts 17:28).

William Blake expressed it this way:

> Think not thou canst sigh a sigh
> and thy Maker is not by;
> Think not thou canst weep a tear
> and thy Maker is not near.

For the Christian, then, the practice of the presence of God is not the projecting of some imaginary object from within one's own mind and then seeking to realize that presence. It is rather the recognition of the real presence of the One who fills the whole universe.

The psalmist confessed that even his innermost thoughts were open to the One who is nearer than breath.

> Where can I go from your Spirit?
> Where can I flee from your presence?
> If I go up to the heavens, you are there;
> if I make my bed in the depths, you are there.
> If I rise on the wings of the dawn,
> if I settle on the far side of the sea,
> even there your hand will guide me,
> your right hand will hold me fast. (Ps 139:7-10)

In his *Letters to Malcolm,* C. S. Lewis says: "We may ignore, but we can nowhere evade, the presence of God. The world is crowded with Him. He walks everywhere *incognito.*"[3] That he does.

This is dangerous ground, I know. The risks probably help explain the widespread neglect of the doctrine of immanence in some Christian circles. Many Christians fear mysticism—and not without reason.

What we must resist are two rivals to the biblical portrait of God: pantheism and deism. When we are among pantheists, who believe that an orchid or a honeybee is part of God, we must insist on God's distinctness. He is other than we, and all created things, are. But when we are among deists, who hold that the Creator is an absentee landlord or an impersonal force, we must stress God's personal presence.

Perhaps the more pervasive reason we neglect the doctrine of God's presence is traceable to the restlessness it brings. He often comes to us not to comfort but to confront. The presence we evade is his presence in wrath.

But isn't that the mark of reality? Deep down we know that nothing that always and everywhere agrees with us can have objective reality. Only sunsets in fantasyland never fade. Only dream lovers never disagree with us—real lovers often do. So with God. He is more real than our dreams.

In the second case, God's presence appears as witness to his saving acts recorded in biblical history. According to Genesis, when Adam and Eve rebelled against God and tried to hide from him, he sought them out in an effort to mend the broken relationship. This pattern persists throughout the pages of the Bible: God, not humankind, makes the overture of love.

God came to Abraham in the land of Ur and called him to a country far from his people. God appeared to the other patriarchs—at times in almost human form—in order to confirm his promise to Abraham and his children. He called the enslaved people of Israel out of Egypt and went before them as a fiery cloud, leading them by fire and smoke to the Promised Land. By creating a tradition of prophetic voices in Israel, God appeared in the spoken word, then in the written Word. Throughout its history Israel recognized the presence of the Lord in clouds and people and Word. From this story of God's persistent presence we can discover several of his dominant personal attributes.

The Love of God

First is the love of God. This is evident many times in the Old Testament, but most clearly in the experiences and the message of the prophets. The Lord often drafted a prophet for sacrificial service and commanded him to demonstrate "the word of the Lord" by some painful experience.

Among the most difficult assignments was Hosea's. God told him to lavish his love on an unworthy woman. The prophet bound her to himself in the marriage covenant. Then he felt the bitterness and pain of her desertion and adultery. The marriage was broken, yet God would not let Hosea forget. He sent him after her. Hosea pursued her and wooed her until she returned to his home.

Through this experience, Hosea preached—and demonstrated— the love of God, love freely and lavishly given, yet squandered and spurned by his truant people. God's love was love that would not let his people go. He persisted until they returned to the privileges of the covenant they had broken.

While we can see the love of God reflected in Hosea's tragic love story, there is a significant difference between human love and God's love. We say that "love is blind"—but never totally. We love because we find something lovable in another. We expect some return for our devotion. But God's love is different. He loves without reasons—at least any reason known to men and women.

This thought appears many times in the Bible. In the book of Deuteronomy, Moses reminds Israel: "The LORD did not set his affection on you and choose you because you were more numerous than other peoples, for you were the fewest of all peoples. But it was because the LORD loved you" (Deut 7:7-8). *I loved you because I loved you.* When we press for reasons we lose the love of God in the mystery of his hidden character. Unlike human love, God's love is undeserved, unconditioned, totally free.

In his *Life of God in the Soul of Man,* seventeenth-century Scottish minister Henry Scougal said, "God hath long contended with a stubborn world, and thrown down many a blessing upon them; and when all his other gifts could not prevail, he at last made a gift of himself."[4] That is God's love.

The Faithfulness of God

The test of such love is in another attribute of God. We call it *faithfulness.* The best reflection of God's faithfulness is again marriage. In wedlock two people create a covenant. They commit themselves to one another "for better or for worse." In all kinds of situations, highs and lows, they promise to be faithful to each other. That is the picture the

Bible uses to portray the faithfulness of God in his covenant, first with Israel and then with the church.

In modern times we define a host of relations by contracts. These are usually for goods or services and for hard cash. The contract, formal or informal, helps to specify failure in these relationships. That is one reason, however, that the terms of a contract cannot adequately express the relation between God and his people, and why the Lord did not establish a contract with Israel or with the church. He established a *covenant*. There is a difference.

Contracts are broken when one of the parties fails to keep his or her promise. If, let us say, a patient fails to keep an appointment with a doctor, the doctor is not obligated to call the house and inquire, "Where are you? Why haven't you shown up for your appointment?" She simply goes on to her next patient and has her appointment secretary take note of the patient's name who failed to keep the appointment. Next time the patient will find it harder to see his doctor, because he broke an informal contract.

According to the Bible, however, the Lord asks: "Can a mother forget the baby at her breast and have no compassion on the child she has borne? Though she may forget, I will not forget you!" (Is 49:15).

The Bible indicates that God's covenant with us is more like a marriage bond or the ties of a parent to her child than it is a doctor's appointment or a purchase agreement. One member's failure does not destroy the relationship. The covenant rests upon the character of the parties. It puts no conditions on faithfulness. It is an unconditional commitment to love and serve.

God's covenant is the heart of his relationship with human beings. Like a human marriage, God's covenant calls for faithfulness. As Israel's history shows, however, the chosen people proved faithless. They turned from the Lord, time and again, and trusted in powerful nations and foreign gods. Israel committed spiritual adultery. Yet even in the face of Israel's infidelity, God proved faithful.

In his book *The Distinctive Ideas of the Old Testament*, Norman Snaith says, "Wonderful as is His love for His covenant people, His steady persistence in it is more wonderful still. The most important of all the distinctive ideas of the Old Testament is God's steady and extraordinary persistence in continuing to love wayward Israel in spite of Israel's insistent waywardness."⁵

Again the contrast with human faithfulness is striking. Human beings are never free from the temptation to unfaithfulness, the infidelity of the heart. Yet when someone proves untrue to us, we are quick to judge. We are ready to punish. But when Israel went too far, and God had to bring judgment upon his people, even then God was true to his promise. A remnant of Israel and Judah survived the exiles. God would not be untrue to himself. He would fulfill his loving purpose for Israel, even when Israel itself was the major roadblock to it.

The Righteousness of God
The consequence of this faithful love of God for humanity introduces a third revealing characteristic of God. We call it *justice* or *righteousness*. Both terms are widely misunderstood. In our day *justice* has come to mean "my rights," while *righteousness* often stands for a stuffy legalism paraded by religious people.

In the Bible, however, the Hebrew terms reveal an unusual side of the character of God. The root of the term suggests whatever "is as it should be." But what can that mean when we say God is righteous? That he plays the game according to the rules? That he is a perfect gentleman? Not exactly. God made the rules. He not only defines what is moral; he is the source of morality. Not only is he righteous; he is concerned that his people be righteous as well. Righteousness is not only a part of his personal character; it is an essential part of his government of the world.

In the Bible, poets, prophets and scribes unite in asserting God's relentless opposition to injustice and the oppression of human beings. God's wrath is against the person who exploits a neighbor. One episode in the life of David, Israel's most illustrious king, graphically illustrates this attribute. David had sinned grievously against God by taking Bathsheba to his bed and then attempting to cover his affair by arranging the death of her husband, Uriah. The sin, however, was not hidden from the prophet of God. Nathan told the king a story about a rich man who seized a poor neighbor's only lamb. And David's anger was kindled. He knew that the poor are not beyond the attention of the righteous God; in fact, they are a special object of God's care. Nathan had only to draw the parallel to Uriah to incite David's repentance.

This care of God for the oppressed is only a step from his deliverance of the oppressed. The righteous God who cares for oppressed people acts to deliver them.

> Who is like you, O LORD?
> You rescue the poor from those too strong for them,
> the poor and needy from those who rob them. (Ps 35:10)

In a world that is not as it should be, the righteous God is at work setting things right. That is simply a reflection of his character.

Christians, then, believe that God is more than a personal impression at death. With the Bible they hold that God is loving and faithful and righteous—like any admirable person, only more so. Much more.

8

THE DARK SIDE
OF LIFE

THE PROBLEM OF EVIL

In the early 1950s Charles Templeton was one of the big names in North American evangelism. While in his twenties he had started preaching at Youth for Christ rallies. From 1951 to 1954 he served as the chief evangelist for the National Council of Churches, preaching to audiences of up to seventy thousand in places such as Soldier's Field in Chicago, the Rose Bowl in Pasadena and Radio City Music Hall in New York City.

In 1957, however, Templeton quit the ministry. He no longer had a message to preach. He entered television and then newspaper journalism before accepting a position as news director for the Canadian Broadcasting Corporation. Quite simply, Charles Templeton had lost his faith.

"I looked at the world," he said in 1978, "and it doesn't seem to me that it bespoke a God that could be described as father. It seems to be a universe indifferent to man and to all creatures." To support this estimate he cited natural disasters such as a typhoon that killed thousands, old and young, and left others unsheltered, diseased and starving. "When I see that kind of prodigal waste," he said, "it doesn't look to me like the act of a father."[1]

Sometimes faith is all uphill. Through the centuries Christians have confessed faith in "God the Father Almighty, Maker of heaven and earth." But is that realistic? There are so many tragic events. If we attribute them all to God, we would seem to make of him a repulsive monster, not a loving Father.

The Barriers to Belief

Is it true that all things have meaning and purpose in God's sight? In the bitter experiences of life, can I believe that God is using these things somehow to work out his purpose? That is the way most people encounter what we usually call "the problem of evil." It is one of the greatest roadblocks to faith.

Alfred, Lord Tennyson, who often longed for the assurance of life's meaning, wrote,

> O, yet we trust that somehow good
> Will be the final goal of ill,
> To pangs of nature, sins of will,
> Defeats of doubt, and taints of blood;
>
> That nothing walks with aimless feet;
> That not one life shall be destroyed,
> Or cast as rubbish to the void,
> When God has made the pile complete.
>
> So runs my dream; but what am I?
> An infant crying in the night;
> An infant crying for the light;
> And with no language but a cry. *(In Memoriam A. H. H.)*

The Loss of the Mysterious

This barrier to belief is not new. The Old Testament prophets and psalmists show clearly that men and women struggled with it in ancient Israel. What makes the argument so powerful today is the social context in which people raise it.

The Western world today, as we have seen, is pervaded by secularism, a style of life and a pattern of thought based upon the assumption that the meaning of life can be discussed and decisions can be made without any reference to God. In a secular world people are conditioned to resist all thoughts of God. We can find several reasons for this.

In the first place, modern men and women seldom think of God because they are preoccupied with secular concerns. Many people are just too busy to worry about the existence of God. This preoccupation is usually a product of affluence. We are swamped by things. Things to see; things to buy; things to finance; things to repair; things to store; things to dump.

Jesus once put his finger on our fevered infection. In his parable about the sower (Mt 13:1-23) he described some people in whom the "worries of this life" choke out the Word of God. Our constant focus on the here-and-now dulls our sense of spiritual reality.

In the second place, modern people find faith in God difficult because they are conditioned to think of the world as though there were no God. Few people today assume that God controls the weather. We all know that atmospheric conditions are caused by high and low pressure systems, humidity levels and wind currents. Who among us trace our illnesses to God's activity? We know all about viruses, carcinogens and cholesterol in our bodies. And we no longer need to assume God's existence for health or healing. We have pills for that.

In the third place, contemporary culture is biased against faith in God because we suffer from atrophy of the sense of wonder. Pioneering scientists seldom lose this sense of awe before the universe, but common people often do. We tend to believe that all the mystery goes out of a flower when botanists name its parts. Or we no longer catch our breath in the light of a dazzling sunset. Television reproduces the scene nightly at five and ten.

These cultural attitudes are so deadening because, as sociologist Peter Berger once pointed out, most of what we "know" we take on the authority of others. Only as others continue to confirm this "knowledge" for us will we accept it as plausible. In Western societies this puts God at a decided disadvantage, because he has been all but banned from public life.[2]

For all these reasons, then, the tragic side of life strikes us as a powerful put-down of faith in God.

Human Responsibility

When suffering comes, it is usually either of two types. Most of our pain comes from human action or inaction. This includes crimes, automobile accidents, wars, broken marriages, some starvation and much of our ill-health. All the great genocides of this century—the Holocaust under Hitler, the purges in the Soviet Union under Stalin and the extermination of Ugandans by Idi Amin—are traceable to human decisions. As a race, human beings show an amazing capacity to inflict suffering upon each other.

Awareness of this violence in human nature by no means solves the problem of pain, but it does demonstrate how often we are perpetrators of pain as well as the victims of it.

A lesser proportion of our suffering comes from so-called natural disasters—earthquakes, cyclones, tidal waves and droughts. In these cases no human being seems directly responsible for the mindless deaths of infants and the lifelong suffering endured by innocent victims.

In those cases where some human being shares in the responsibility for suffering, it may be easier to direct our rage toward another person. But how can God be exempt from blame in the tragedies of nature? If a good and omnipotent God created the world, why is it so full of pain? Perhaps John Stuart Mill, the philosopher, posed the problem in its sharpest terms: "If God is able to prevent evil and does not, he is not good. If he would prevent evil and cannot, he is not almighty."[3]

Many, like Charles Templeton, have felt this dilemma so deeply that they have renounced their faith and have chosen instead some form of courageous unbelief. But what sort of unbelief is this that continues to point a finger at God, even while denying his existence? Doesn't genuine unbelief stop complaining and simply accept a meaningless universe?

C. S. Lewis found this so. While attempting to deny the existence of God during his student days, he discovered a major flaw in his argument. "My argument against God," he explained, "was that the universe seemed so cruel and unjust. But how had I got this idea of *just* and *unjust?* A man does not call a line crooked unless he has some idea of a straight line. . . . Thus in the very act of trying to prove that God did not exist—in other words, that the whole of reality was senseless—I found I was forced to assume that one part of reality— namely my idea of justice—was full of sense."[4]

Angry atheism, it turns out, is too simple. If the universe is without meaning, then we would never find it out. True atheists do not argue with God about right and wrong. They do not believe such things exist. So unbelief is not a productive approach to the problem of pain.

God's Presence in Pain

The Christian faith—so far as I have been able to determine—has only a partial answer to the problem of evil. A great deal of mystery remains. Most Christians, however, lean upon several fundamental truths.

First, Christianity acknowledges the reality of evil. When Jesus taught his disciples to pray, he included the petition "Deliver us from evil." The Christian faith, unlike some other religions, never regards evil as an illusion. It is not a misguided way of thinking, a problem of human perception of reality. It is there, an actual fact of human existence.

At the same time, Christianity has never endorsed a doctrine of dualism—a view of reality that holds two conflicting eternal principles: one good, the other evil. This dogma appears in some ancient religions such as Manichaeanism and Gnosticism. But whatever Christians have done with the image of Satan, they have expressed few doubts that he is limited in his evil activities by the power of Almighty God.

In brief, then, Christians insist that evil is real. It is not some sort of collective nightmare that will eventually vanish. But neither is it ultimate. Only God is ultimate. And for his own mysterious reasons God allows evil to operate.

Second, Christianity teaches that men and women are endowed by God with a fundamental freedom. By that term we do not mean that men and women can do what they wish. They are limited by their finite existence. By "freedom" Christians mean that men and women are responsible before God for their lives. They are free from excessive external constraints to good or evil. They are not helpless victims of heredity or environment. They are responsible for their choices.

This reminder of my responsibility for my life tends to shift the problem of evil a bit. It takes it out of the realm of theories and makes it a personal matter. That is what Jesus did. Some of his contemporaries pointed to a recent tragedy: a group of Galileans were in the temple offering sacrifice when Herod's soldiers suddenly fell upon them and slaughtered them on the spot. How could God let that happen? And what did Jesus say? He said, "Do you think these Galileans were worse sinners than all the other Galileans because they suffered this way? I tell you, no! But unless you repent, you too will all perish" (Lk 13:1-5).

Notice how Jesus shifted the question from "God, how could you let this happen?" to "God, why doesn't it happen to me?" He brought his curious listeners to their own responsibility before God. He would not let them use the problem of evil as a cover for their own sin. We all tend to forget that we ourselves are part of the problem of evil.

Third, the Scriptures speak of a God who is moved by human suffering. He is not a heartless observer. He cares and comes to sufferers' aid. At the end of his prophecy, Habakkuk, who had wrestled so vigorously with the problem of pain, wrote,

> Though the fig tree does not bud
>> and there are no grapes on the vines,
> though the olive crop fails
>> and the fields produce no food,
> though there are no sheep in the pen
>> and no cattle in the stalls,
> yet I will rejoice in the LORD,
>> I will be joyful in God my Savior. (Hab 3:17-18)

Much later, Jesus, aware of his own approaching agony, told his disciples, "In this world you will have trouble. But take heart! I have overcome the world" (Jn 16:33).

Christians have always found this victory in Jesus' cross. There, faith says, God entered into the travail of sin and suffering and moved decisively for our salvation. Because of this crucial act, men and women can find assurance of God's presence and power in dark valleys of pain.

What God gives his people is not answers; he gives them his presence. That is what the book of Job illustrates so effectively. Job wanted an answer to the problem of the suffering of the righteous. The book shows that the struggle was unfolding on two levels—an earthly level and a heavenly level. Job had no access to the heavens. And God never told him about the heavenly level. Instead, he came to Job. So the climax of the book resounds in Job's words: "My ears had heard of you but now my eyes have seen you" (Job 42:5).

Finally, Christianity promises a life to come where justice will prevail. Without this hope, the problem of evil might well be insoluble. But the Christian hope is not something added to faith; it is part of faith's substance. The mysteries of tragedy, evil, pain and injustice are not resolved in this life. At present we do not see everything subject to God. But we see Jesus. He is the promise of the life to come.

Faith and the Future
In the end, then, it is not the mere presence of pain that makes faith

in God difficult. Otherwise, people would find it difficult to believe in God because of the discomfort they feel in carrying their own groceries from the store. What does bother us is the occurrence of evil on a scale so great that we cannot imagine anything that would compensate for it.

The patient in the dentist's waiting room has little difficulty imagining the time when her suffering will prove worthwhile. But one's three-year-old grandson's dying of cancer is another matter. We find it more difficult to imagine any situation that could justify that pain. Even God, we feel, cannot make *that* not matter. The real problem of evil comes when we witness or experience pain so great that we can't imagine any way that even God could justify it.

But let us suppose—just suppose—that God's resources are so much beyond what I can imagine that he can produce a situation in which I can honestly say, "I see now that my personal pain at the loss of my son in this tragedy fits into a plan for a much greater good than my personal happiness at this moment."[5]

This line of thought does not solve the problem of evil. But it points in the direction of a solution. The idea goes back to Jesus. "A woman giving birth to a child," he once said, "has pain because her time has come; but when her baby is born she forgets the anguish because of her joy that a child is born into the world" (Jn 16:21).

William Cowper, a hymn writer who encountered the problem of evil personally and profoundly, wrote,

> God moves in a mysterious way
> His wonders to perform;
> He plants His footsteps in the sea,
> And rides upon the storm.

> Judge not the Lord by feeble sense,
> But trust Him for His grace;
> Behind a frowning providence
> He hides a smiling face.

The problem of evil, then, is the problem of faith. Do we believe in a God big enough to make any suffering seem worthwhile? The overwhelming testimony of the Bible is that when countless men and women living in ancient times encountered the painful side of life, just as we do, they anchored their lives to just such a faith.

9
THE INVASION
JESUS CHRIST

The world's major religions trace their origins to a few great leaders. The figures of Buddha, Moses, Muhammad and Christ tower over the faiths of the world's people. The vast majority of people on earth have been influenced by these religious leaders.

Even the simplest introduction to these faiths, however, reveals that the place of the leader in the religion varies greatly. The Buddha (Siddartha Gautama) is the most elusive of the founders. His influence among Buddhists is limited to his teaching. His life and personal history are almost incidental. Moses stands out as a major figure in Jewish religion, but Jews would never think of pointing to Moses as the founder of their religion. Muhammad is the supreme prophet of the Muslim world, and his teachings are the authoritative voice for Islam, but no Muslim would refer to Muhammad as "Lord" or "Savior."

Obviously, Jesus Christ's relation to Christianity is unique. He is central. Only in Christianity is the personality of the founder absolutely essential to the faith. Remove Jesus Christ from Christianity, prove that the gospel story is a myth, and the Christian faith crumbles into worthless dust. You might retain an ethical system of some sort, but the controlling influence that Christianity has had over the lives of Christians during the last two thousand years would be gone.

Why? What makes Jesus Christ central to Christianity? Who do Christians say he is? The answer to that question pierces to the heart of the Christian message. The church in every century, and in every place, has not only followed his teachings. It has worshiped him as a living Lord.

If we stop and think about that fact for a minute we may feel the shock of it, just as Jesus' earliest followers did. C. S. Lewis put it best:

Among the Jews there suddenly turns up a man who goes about talking as if He was God. . . . Now let us get this clear. Among Pantheists, like the Indians, anyone might say that he was a part of God, or one with God: There would be nothing very odd about it. But this man, since He was a Jew, could not mean that kind of God. God, in their language, meant the Being outside the world Who had made it and was infinitely different from anything else. And when you have grasped that, you will see that what this man said was, quite simply, the most shocking thing that has ever been uttered by human lips.[1]

The Life of Christ

Outwardly, Jesus' life was like thousands of other lives in the land of Palestine during the era of Roman occupation. He was born in the village of Bethlehem and was reared in a Galilean town called Naza-reth. Like most eldest sons in those days, he was probably apprenticed in the family trade—in his case carpentry.

A time came, however, when he left home to travel about Galilee, Samaria and Judea—the three districts of Palestine— preaching, heal-ing and teaching. He joined the ranks of itinerating rabbis in Israel. His career, however, proved brief and tragic. He ended up on a Ro-man cross outside Jerusalem at Passover time.

The simplicity of the story only accents the urgency of the question:

Why did people come to worship Jesus of Nazareth? Some historians have tried to present Jesus as just another Jewish rabbi. That is surely the place to start. He was Jewish, and people did consider him "a teacher sent from God." But we cannot make Jesus intelligible until we also see him as the instigator of the Christian movement.

The Claims of Christ

Strangely, the Jesus movement began with some things Jesus said and did that most Jews considered blasphemy. The word is not too strong. It suggests defamation or injury to the reputation of God. That fits, because many of the things Jesus said and did were shocking to religious people. He spoke of God in the most intimate terms and claimed to have unique divine authority.

Take, for example, his habit of referring to God as *Abba*. In his native language, Aramaic, that meant *Daddy*. He used the expression in his own prayers, and he taught his followers to use it in theirs (Mk 14:36; Mt 6:9).

Most pious Jews found that chumminess shocking. They knew the commandment against taking God's name in vain, and they had come to hold God's name so sacred that they never spoke it aloud. They chose to refer to God in polite euphemisms such as "He Whose Name Makes the Hair on the Back of the Neck Stand on End." Rabbinic law held that anyone heard uttering the name of God aloud was to be stoned to death for blasphemy. Yet that was the culture in which Jesus used a family nickname—Abba—to refer to God.

Jesus reflected a similarly shocking attitude toward Jewish customs. Take sabbath observance. The Jews considered the sabbath a holy day. One sabbath, however, Jesus and his disciples were hiking through a field of grain. When they grew hungry, they dared to pick some of the grain to eat. The religious authorities caught them in the act and demanded an explanation.

Jesus answered that King David had sanctioned a similar action of his companions. After all, said Jesus, the sabbath was made for people, not people for the sabbath. "The Son of Man is Lord of the

Sabbath" (Mt 12:8). Was he claiming authority over the sabbath? Isn't
that a clear case of blasphemy?

Take one more provocative act, Jesus' practice of forgiving people's
sins. According to the Old Testament, only God can forgive sins
against God's law. And yet once when Jesus returned to his home-
town, some men brought to him a paralytic man lying on a mat. When
Jesus saw the man he said to him: "Take heart, son; your sins are
forgiven" (Mt 9:1-3). You can imagine what the teachers of the law
thought: "This is blasphemy."

Jesus' conflict with traditional religion in Israel came into sharpest
focus in Pharisaism. The Pharisees were diligent students of the Scriptures. They were convinced believers in God. They were determined
that their traditions should be obeyed in the tiniest detail. But somehow, in spite of their passionate devotion to the Law, they had lost
touch with the living God. Religion had become for them a perfor-
mance of rituals and duties aimed at gaining God's favor. Anyone
unwilling to conform to their concept of religion fell under their scorn.
They had come to think of God as a heartless taskmaster rather than
a caring Father. Pharisaism illustrates how easy it is for any religion
to become an obstacle rather than a highway to God.

Jesus never revolted against this Judaism offhandedly. He tried to
remain a loyal son of Israel, but he could not allow the damaging
effects of Pharisaism to go unchallenged. It stood in the way of men
and women's seeing God as a gracious and forgiving Father.

Jesus, however, was more than a religious reformer. He dared to
confront the Pharisees because he claimed an authority higher than
their traditions. Jesus was convinced that he was the Savior of the
world. In him men and women would find a new and living way to
God. "I am the light of the world," he said (Jn 8:12). "I am the way
and the truth and the life" (Jn 14:6). Constantly he claimed to stand
at the center of life. "Come to me," he said, "all you who are weary
and burdened, and I will give you rest" (Mt 11:28).

When we compare these words with the promises of the prophets
in Israel, we see that Jesus was assuming a position that only God can

take. Our estimation of Jesus cannot ignore this claim. If Jesus is mistaken in this central conviction, then we must consider him an egotistical religious teacher—sincere perhaps, but fundamentally misguided. Misguided to the point of insanity.

But when we survey Jesus' life and teachings we find no trace of such egotism. He sets himself at the center of life, not for selfish or deranged purposes, but because he humbly recognizes that in the eternal order of reality he belongs there.

Christ's Impact

This claim to divine authority was more than a personal psychological quirk. Hundreds of people who crossed Jesus' path recognized it as true. They found themselves confronted by a major decision. Would they join the scoffers who dismissed him as a troublesome dreamer, or would they follow him to God and be transformed?

After a wealthy tax collector named Zacchaeus invited Jesus to his home, Zacchaeus found he had to reorder his whole lifestyle, beginning with the way he valued his money. When he expressed his willingness to change, Jesus said to him: "Today salvation has come to this house" (Lk 19:1-9).

Such encounters were almost common. Peter, one of the disciples who had seen scores of men and women turned around by their encounters with Jesus, tried to express what he had come to think of Jesus. It was almost the unthinkable thought. But under Jesus' questioning he blurted out, "You are the Christ, the Son of the living God" (Mt 16:13-16). Jesus didn't deny it.

In our tolerant age men and women have tried to present Christianity as something charming and popular. They have painted Jesus as a religious teacher with unusual insight into human nature, but one without offense. That is absurd, for Christ went about Galilee giving offense to all kinds of people. This young Jew was so inflammatory in his message that he was thrown out of synagogues, hounded from place to place and finally arrested as a public nuisance.

"Let us," Dorothy Sayers once said, "in Heaven's name, drag out the Divine Drama from under the dreadful accumulation of slipshod thinking and trashy sentiment heaped upon it, and set it on an open stage to startle the world into some sort of vigorous reaction."² The Christian centuries echo with a resounding "Amen!"

Jesus' ministry among men and women reached a climax in his death, which secured for him his unique place in Christianity. For him death came as no surprise. He apparently expected the opposition of the Jewish authorities to lead to his destiny. More than once he mentioned his approaching death to his disciples. He seemed to anticipate his shameful treatment in Jerusalem. He knew his claim to divine authority was not a popular one. At his trial the Jewish leaders told the Roman governor, "We have a law, and according to that law he must die, because he claimed to be the Son of God" (Jn 19:7).

When the crucifixion came, though, it struck his disciples as a tragic enigma. Death somehow seemed a contradiction to the life of Jesus. He had been so often the victor. Why was he now so obviously death's victim?

The disciples discovered the answer to that question in the surprising sequel to the crucifixion, Jesus' resurrection from the grave. After three days in the tomb, he returned to them. On several occasions he offered them proof that death could not hold him. They saw then the significance of the cross. This extraordinary thing was nothing less than an act of God. Jesus died an atoning sacrifice for the sins of men and women and was raised again to life by the power of God in order to provide forgiveness and spiritual power for all who believe in him.

On the day of Pentecost, when the Holy Spirit descended upon the disciples and empowered them to witness boldly of the significance of Jesus' life, death and resurrection, Peter dared to tell his Jewish kinfolk, "God has made this Jesus, whom you crucified, both Lord and Christ" (Acts 2:36).

So the Christian gospel was born. As the Anglican scholar Michael Green once put it, the disciples believed that within the confines of a human life "the Ultimate had become embodied, the Absolute had become contemporary."[3] The Lord of the Hidden World had visited ours.

Faith in Jesus as a supernatural Savior courses through the twenty-seven books of the New Testament and makes them one in witness and intent. One passage from the apostle Paul, perhaps based on an early Christian hymn, will speak for hundreds of other texts in praising the unique nature and accomplishment of Jesus:

Who, being in very nature God,
did not consider equality with God something to be grasped,
but made himself nothing,
taking the very nature of a servant,
being made in human likeness.
And being found in appearance as a man,
he humbled himself
and became obedient to death—even death on a cross!
Therefore God exalted him to the highest place
and gave him the name that is above every name,
that at the name of Jesus every knee should bow,
in heaven and on earth and under the earth,
and every tongue confess that Jesus Christ is Lord,
to the glory of God the Father. (Phil 2:6-11)

The Birth of Christology

After the passing of the apostles, during the early centuries of church history, Christian believers faced a disturbing problem: How do we describe this profound reality we call "God in flesh"? Believers quickly discovered that it is all too easy to fall into some misleading answers to that question.

On the one hand, if they answered that Jesus was some divine being, then their simple logic forced them to add that Jesus only *seemed* to be a human being. Stories of gods' disguising themselves in human form, coming to earth to accomplish this or that divine mission and then returning to the divine realm were too common in the ancient world to be ignored.

Was Jesus born of a virgin? So were half the members of the Pantheon. Was Jesus ascended to heaven? So was Hercules. Jesus, it seemed, fit the pattern of the Greek gods. So some misguided believers said that Jesus only seemed to be a man; he was really a god of some sort.

But thoughtful Christians rejected such views and labeled them *Docetic*—from the Greek word *dokein,* meaning "to seem" or "to appear." They recognized the problem with this line of thinking. It undercuts the gospel.

If Jesus only appeared to be human and never really lived among men and women, if he was a ghost, then the gospel is reduced to a myth. After all, that is what the stories of the Greek gods were. Only a child might take them as factual. But the gospel means "good news." Christians were claiming that in the life of Jesus—a historical person who had been known by thousands of people—God had actually entered history and provided salvation for humankind.

On the other hand, some early would-be Christians answered the question about Jesus by insisting that he was really and fully human. God had simply empowered him by a special gift of his Spirit. This view is called *adoptionism* because it holds that God adopted Jesus for his purposes.

That, too, was plausible. It had certain passages in the New Testament to support it. We can think of instances when Jesus was angry or hungry or tired. The Gospels speak of his growing up through childhood and adolescence, of his eating and drinking, of his death and burial. So in the early church there were those who professed Christianity who insisted that the answer to the "Who is Jesus?" question was "A man, only a man."

The trouble with this view is that it, too, empties the gospel of its power. If the person who died on the cross was only a human being, then his death could only be a tragic accident. He might be a model of selfless dedication, a devotee of noble ideals who inspires others to similar nobility, a kind of Jewish Socrates. But he would still be nothing more than an example.

If that were so, then where is the good news for sinners? Where is the atonement for sin? Where is the overthrow of evil? The church rejected this view of Jesus, just as it had the opposite teaching of the Docetists. It examined the portrait in terms of the gospel and found it a distortion.

The classical Christian teaching about Christ—called Christology—developed through a lengthy process culminating in the middle of the fifth century. A series of church councils worked through a maze created by a number of well-meaning Christian thinkers. The resulting doctrine of Christ makes no logical or mathematical sense, but it wasn't supposed to.

The climactic council at Chalcedon in Asia Minor (today's Turkey) asserted that Jesus was completely and fully human. It also affirmed that Jesus was completely and fully God. Finally, the council confessed that this total man and this total God was one completely normal person. In other words, Jesus combined two natures, human and divine, in one unique person.

One of the finest elaborations of this truth came from Leo, the bishop of Rome. "The properties of each nature," he wrote, giving his views to the council, "were preserved entire, and came together to form one person. Humility was assumed by majesty, weakness by strength, mortality by eternity; and to pay the debt that we incurred, an inviolable nature was united to a nature that can suffer." The Lord of the universe allowed his infinite majesty to be overshadowed, and took upon himself the form of a servant. The Immortal One submitted to the laws of death.[4]

This classical, orthodox affirmation from Chalcedon made it possible to tell the story of Jesus as good news. Since Jesus was a normal human being, bone of our bone and flesh of our flesh, he could fulfill every demand of God's moral law, and he could suffer and die a real death. Since he was truly God, his death was capable of satisfying divine justice. God himself had provided the sacrifice.

The difficulty with this Christology is its absolute uniqueness. According to normal human standards, it makes no sense. It doesn't add up. One human being plus one God does not equal one person. Certainly not in any ordinary sense. But then Christians are not claiming that Jesus was ordinary.

In spite of all its difficulties, this view of Jesus enables us to insist that he died a real, fully human death, and at the same time to believe that his death secured the necessary benefits for human beings. Christians hold that it provides an acceptable answer to the question "Who is Jesus?"

The Worship of Christ

This witness to Jesus' unique role in God's plan of salvation is more than the brainchild of some Greek theologians assembled in solemn councils. It echoes the convictions of worshiping Christian congregations across the centuries and around the globe today. It resounds in the adoring praise of the church. "Out of the overflow of the heart the mouth speaks" (Mt 12:34).

Richard Hooker, the Anglican divine, once said, "Our safest eloquence concerning him is in our silence." But surely our second greatest eloquence comes in song. A deep instinct has always inspired the church to sing of the mystery of the incarnate Word. The living church is not so much a school of people holding all the correct doctrines as a worshiping congregation of God's people.[5]

Open any Christian hymnbook and check the great hymns, phrase upon phrase, and the impact is unmistakable:

> O for a thousand tongues to sing
> My great Redeemer's praise,
> The glories of my God and King . . .

> Kyrie eleison,
> Christe eleison,
> Kyrie eleison.
> [Lord have mercy; Christ have mercy; Lord have mercy.]

> Crown him the Lord of heaven,
> One with the Father known. . . .

> All hail, Redeemer, hail!
> For Thou hast died for me;
> Thy praise and glory shall not fail
> Throughout eternity.

The language demonstrates that in the presence of Jesus Christ Christian people maintain an attitude of mind, a spirit of submission, that can only be called worship. If Michelangelo were to enter our living room, we would rise to greet him. But if Jesus Christ were to enter, we would fall down and worship him. He is more than a model or a teacher. He is God incarnate and reigning Lord.

Christians today are tempted to abandon this exclusive view of Jesus. Respect for other religions compels them to question the New Testament portrait of the Lord Jesus Christ. It seems more modest to speak of Christianity as "the religion of Western people." But that temptation is self-defeating. Such a view destroys the heart of the Christian faith. For the New Testament's universal Savior it substitutes a religion that Jesus and the apostles—as well as the orthodox believers of all ages— would criticize as quickly as they did alternative religions of their own times.

Students of world religions often compare true faith to a mountain peak. The trails to the top, they say, all start at the base of the mountain and wind their own ways to the summit, converging as they draw near the top. So those who climb the mountain come closer to each other the farther they climb. On the summit they all, at last, see the same God.

Christians, however, insist that none has stood upon that summit except Jesus Christ.

10

THE AGONY
AND THE ANSWER
THE CROSS

The *Lion, the Witch and the Wardrobe* is a children's story by C. S. Lewis. Four youngsters from England find themselves transported magically to the land of Narnia, a fascinating world where fauns and beavers talk and plan just like people. The creator of Narnia is Aslan, the great and powerful lion. But when the children arrive, Narnia is under the influence of a wicked White Witch.

One of the children, Edmund, turns against his brother and sisters and joins forces with the Witch. In order to save him, Aslan gives himself to be killed in Edmund's place. He surrenders to the White Witch and her evil Hags. They bind him on a great Stone Table and slay him.

The next day Edmund's sisters, Susan and Lucy, stare in disbelief at the empty table and at Aslan, alive and strong.

"But what does it all mean?" asks Susan, finally satisfied that Aslan is not a ghost.

"It means," Aslan explains, "that though the Witch knew the Deep Magic, there is a magic deeper still which she did not know. . . . If she could have looked a little further back, . . . she would have known that when a willing victim who had committed no treachery was killed in a traitor's stead, the Table would crack and Death itself would start working backwards."[1]

Death itself would start working backwards! That is the Christian faith. The death and resurrection of Jesus Christ have set in motion a process that runs counter to the direction of life around us.

"After desire has conceived," the Bible says, "it gives birth to sin; and sin, when it is full-grown, gives birth to death" (Jas 1:15). That is the downward course of humanity. But Christ has brought life and immortality to light through the gospel. And the cross on which Jesus died starts death working backwards.

The Crucifixion

It is possible to look at the cross from a purely historical perspective. Crucifixion was a common penalty for criminals in Roman times. It was probably the Persians who had introduced this shocking form of execution, but the Romans seized the gruesome practice in order to rid themselves of terrorists, slaves and hardened criminals.

The victim usually endured a merciless scourging with straps laced with thorns or jagged bits of bone. During the beating the soldiers charged with the execution often indulged their bestial emotions. Some victims died from the flogging alone. Jesus survived.

After the beating, the soldiers bound or nailed the victim to a rough beam, the horizontal log for the cross. Burdened with this, the prisoner had to drag himself through the streets to the place of execution. There soldiers lifted the cross-beam, bearing the victim, and secured it to the vertical post. Finally, the soldiers nailed the feet to the cross. Time did the rest—fever, shock, thirst, pain, delirium and death.

This was Jesus' destiny because he had inflamed the hatred of the Jewish authorities. His contempt of Jewish traditions and his claims of divine powers brought him at last to the Sanhedrin, the religious high court. These enraged men condemned him to death for blasphemy. According to the Mosaic law, that meant death by stoning.

Rome, however, did not grant the Jews the power to carry out executions. So the Jewish authorities whisked Jesus away to the Roman governor, Pontius Pilate.

"We have found this man subverting our nation," they cried. "He opposes payment of taxes to Caesar and claims to be Christ, a king" (Lk 23:2).

In order to gain the death penalty, the religious authorities, while spiriting Jesus through the darkened city's streets, had shifted the charge against him. Before Pilate, Jesus was a rabble-rouser, a conspirator. The charge was high treason. Pilate tried to sidestep the death penalty, but under pressure he eventually crumbled and gave the order: "Crucify him." On one level, that is the story of the cross.

There is, however, another level of meaning in these events, a level that the historian usually refuses to enter. We enter it, however, when we ask, What was God doing in these events? That is another matter. On the surface, the cross has all the signs of a judicial murder. But on another level of meaning—the level on which the Bible discusses it—the cross reveals an unbelievable gospel.

The Gospel of the Cross

I call it a gospel because it is astoundingly good news. The cross says men and women can now find forgiveness with God. Apart from the rescue mission of God, we were like helpless sailors drifting aimlessly at sea in a leaking lifeboat. Our only hope was in the appearance of someone from outside our little world. And that is what the cross reveals. A rescue party has come from the Hidden World.

Basic to the Christian view of the cross, then, is a concept of God. So long as we think of God as some vague, distant force, we will never see the need for reconciliation between God and human creatures. Or if we insist on a God who only loves, who knows neither holiness nor wrath, the cross will never make sense to us—not any Christian sense.

In that view we are asking God to be what we despise in persons. The man or woman who cannot express anger cannot truly love. The person who dismisses treachery or infidelity with a wave of the hand, as if it were nothing, cannot be a true friend or a true spouse. That will never do. In God love and holiness must somehow harmonize.

Surely deep within us there lies a sense that all is not right with God and something ought to be done about it. Why do we make our resolutions? Why do we try to be better men and women? We sense that we are not what we ought to be. Sometimes we tell our analyst about it. Sometimes we try to atone for our failures and sins. Sometimes we deaden the pain with drugs.

This gulf between us and God is not merely an intellectual one, as though the right course on ethics or the right book on religion could fill it. No, the real gulf is in the spiritual realm. We are separated from God by sin in our lives. And that sin deserves God's wrath, God's condemnation. If we refuse to hear of God's holiness, we will never understand Jesus Christ or his cross.

Evidently Jesus saw his whole life and ministry in terms of his end. The words he heard at his baptism, for example, are a key to his understanding of the Old Testament. As Jesus came up out of the water, he heard a voice: "You are my Son, whom I love; with you I am well pleased" (Lk 3:22).

"You are my Son" comes from Psalm 2. "With you I am well pleased" is an echo of Isaiah 42. Together these phrases indicate that Jesus considered himself the fulfillment of Israel's hope for a Messiah, the prophetic Servant of the Lord.

But if Jesus saw his own mission in terms of these prophetic passages, what must he have thought when Isaiah 53 lay open before him? Did he also read, "Surely he took up our infirmities and carried our sorrows" (v. 4) and know that this was the reason he had come into the world?

During long hours Jesus must have turned over and over in his mind the significance of the prophets' words for the days that lay ahead of him. Apparently from the beginning he had seen the end of the road and had counted the cost. He saw his approaching death as a bitter necessity. Messiahship meant taking up the cross.

Why else was he baptized by John? Though he was no transgressor, he was numbering himself with the transgressors (Is 53:12). He was taking the burden of human sin as though it were his own. A mother or father whose son has fallen into some shameful crime can understand. Because of their love for their child, they too enter into the guilt of another. It is not their sin, but they feel the shame of it as though it were their own.

Jesus, however, did more than feel the pain and shame of human sin. He actually endured the punishment for it. He met the demands of justice. He removed every impediment to God's forgiveness.

In the New Testament the central purpose of the death of Christ is clear enough: "God was reconciling the world to himself in Christ, not counting men's sins against them" (2 Cor 5:19). God and people were once estranged from each other, but the cross removed that barrier. It restored sinful people to a holy God.

The term for this reconciliation is *atonement*. William Tyndale, the English Bible translator, was probably the first person to use the term. He wanted to stress that Christ's death made possible the *at-one-ment* of human rebels and a holy God. That much is clear in the New Testament.

Views of the Atonement

Christians have often differed with each other over the detailed explanations of the atonement. Some of them have considered the death of Jesus a ransom paid to Satan in order to gain the release of human beings from Satan's power. Satan captured Jesus in death but was surprised to find at Jesus' resurrection that he had gotten more than he could handle. This is the so-called ransom theory: Jesus' death was the ransom paid to Satan in order to release imprisoned sinners.

Other Christians have described the atonement in terms of a payment owed to God. Human sin, they say, is the failure to give to God the honor he rightly deserves. Dishonor is sin, but since God is infinite, his honor takes on infinite proportions. Human debt, then, is infinite. This is the dilemma: men and women *must* pay God his due; but no human being *can* pay God his due. Since only humans must pay the debt and only God can pay the debt, what humanity needs is a God-man. That is why, in mercy, God sent Jesus to make satisfaction for sin. He paid the debt we owe to God. This is the satisfaction theory of the atonement.

Still other Christians explain reconciliation in terms of the effect of the cross upon people. The example of a suffering Jesus arouses within us a deep admiration of him. We find the meaning of sacrificial love when we see it demonstrated so graphically on the cross, and we are moved by Jesus' example to love others who may at first appear to us as undeserving of the slightest favor. When we love as he loved, we are drawn to God. This is the so-called moral influence theory of the atonement.

The New Testament, however, offers no single theory of the atonement. It presents, instead, a series of dramatic word pictures to magnify the significance of Jesus' death:

We were in hopeless debt, and Jesus paid the debt for us (Lk 7:41-50).

We were slaves, and Jesus came to the marketplace to redeem us from bondage (Eph 1:7).

We were condemned criminals before the judgment seat of God, and Jesus bore our penalty in order to set us free (Rom 15:16).

We were unclean Gentiles, excluded by our sin from the presence of God in the temple, and Jesus gave himself as a sacrifice to consecrate a way for us to approach the throne of mercy (Eph 2:13-14).

We were children in disgrace, far from home, and Jesus brought us back to the family circle (Eph 2:18-19).

We were captives confined to the fortress of Satan, and Jesus broke in to deliver us (Col 2:15).

The terminology and imagery of the bank, the slave market, the law court, the temple, the home and the battlefield are all pressed into the service of the gospel in order to throw light on the atonement of Christ. The cross destroyed the barrier between humankind and God. That is the point.

What thou, my Lord, hast suffered
Was all for sinners' gain;
Mine, mine was the transgression,
But thine the deadly pain.

In his little book *On Christian Truth* Harry Blamires suggests that we think of the human race as if it were flying through time aboard a hijacked jetliner. "God himself directed its takeoff from the divine control-tower. The initiator of all evil, whom we call the Devil, managed to get a boarding pass." When the plane reached its cruising altitude, the devil produced his weapons, threatened the pilot and took control of the aircraft and all its passengers.

Thus the plane hopped on fearfully through history from airport to airport until "it was caught on the tarmac at Jerusalem, an outpost of the Roman empire, in the reign of Tiberius Caesar, where the Son of God offered himself as sole hostage in exchange for passengers and crew."[2] Airplane hijacking has become so common in recent years that it serves well to bring an old truth up to date.

The meaning of the cross was not at first self-evident. Its significance appeared only after the resurrection of Jesus. Jesus' resurrection from the grave is like the finishing touch of a great artist. In a painting, a master may allow his full plan to remain hidden until the last stroke of the brush. Every brush mark suggests the meaning, but its fullness never appears until the artist is done. That last touch brings the significance to every detail of the picture. So it is with the resurrection. We do not understand Jesus, nor do we understand the cross until we see it in the light of the resurrection.

The Resurrection

To many people Jesus' resurrection is the most incredible claim of the Christian faith. It is not the kind of thing, they say, that happens in our world. They know that if someone rushed up to them and announced that some friend of theirs had died three days before and had been buried, but had appeared for breakfast that morning, they would be inclined to question the informer's sanity.

Christians, then, need to explain why they believe that Jesus actually passed through death to the Hidden World and returned for a time to talk about it. Belief in Jesus' resurrection rests on three pieces of evidence: the appearances of Jesus to his disciples, the empty tomb and the subsequent history of the Christian church.

The Gospels indicate that Jesus appeared on many occasions and to a large number of people—five hundred at one time. The records assure us that some of these people were at first quite incredulous. They were not easily convinced. If these appearances were not genuine, we must still explain the accounts.

Some have suggested that the appearances of Christ after the resurrection were merely psychic phenomena. But if that were so, we would expect the conviction that Jesus was alive to grow progressively less vivid once the disciples ceased to be "in touch" with the Hidden World, and we would expect the followers who had not seen the evidence to be as skeptical as third parties usually are when confronted with reports of communications from the dead.

Neither of these expectations, however, corresponds with the facts. The conviction about the resurrection became even more settled once the appearances ceased, and those who had not seen the risen Christ were won to a living faith just as those who had seen. The early Christian witnesses of the resurrection spoke not so much of some past appearance of Christ as of their own experience with the living Savior.[3]

The only other possible explanation is that the empty tomb and the whole series of appearances were a gigantic hoax. But as G. B. Caird once asked, which of the disciples of Jesus, who had been scattered and disillusioned on Good Friday, could by Easter Day have planned and executed so elaborate and so successful a deception? The most likely response to such a trick would have been derisive laughter. Are we really to believe that people will die for a hoax? This supposed hoax deceived several thousand people and has been perpetuated for two thousand years. On the whole, it seems easier to believe the testimony of Peter, John and the rest than to accept either of these explanations.[4]

Evidence for the Resurrection

The decisive evidence for the resurrection, however, is the impact it had on the lives of flesh-and-blood people. On Good Friday, Peter was a broken man, overwhelmed with a sense of shame at having denied Jesus in his hour of crisis. Within a few weeks, however, we find him standing before the Jewish authorities declaring under threat of persecution that "salvation is found in no one else, for there is no other name under heaven given to men by which we must be saved" (Acts 4:12). Something happened in the interval to transform a coward into a hero.

At one point the disciples were meeting in a locked room for fear of the Jews, and something happened to send them out across the world with a burning zeal that no hardship could quench. Paul was persecuting the church, and something happened to make him its greatest missionary. The history of Christianity is simply full of examples of similar transformations, and nothing less than the resurrection will explain them.

For the apostles the resurrection of Jesus was the last stroke of God's brush, the final disclosure of God's presence and mission in the life of Jesus. What had been hidden from them in his lifetime was revealed to them after his death.

As James Smart once pointed out, Jesus' death stripped the disciples of all false expectations about the Messiah, and his resurrection opened their eyes to what Jesus had been about from his first day among them. It revealed to them the climactic fulfillment of the purpose of God which bound all their past history together. They discovered that even the Old Testament spoke of a Messiah who, through death and resurrection, would inaugurate God's rule over stubbornly resistant men and women.[5]

The resurrection, then, was the final proof that Jesus had conquered humanity's last enemy, death. He had shown beyond any possible doubt that his saving victory was complete. Death had started working backwards. To live again was no pious hope or wishful thought; it was a certainty.

11

THE BLUE-COLLAR DEITY

THE HOLY SPIRIT

During what may have been ancient Israel's greatest crisis of faith—the time of the exile—the prophet Ezekiel served as a pastor to his displaced people. The refugees in Babylon had the paralyzing feeling that they were the doomed heirs of the past. "Don't you believe it," said Ezekiel. "God has plans for you."

Ezekiel's response was based upon a vision God had given him. He found himself in a valley of bleached and awesome bones. Apparently, some army had fallen in battle—victims of a swift and successful ambush. Time, vultures and the Near Eastern sun had done the rest. The last signs of life had dried in the summer heat.

"Son of man," Ezekiel heard, "can these bones live?"

"O Sovereign LORD," he responded, "you alone know."

"Prophesy!" the Voice said. "Prophesy to these bones and say to them, 'Dry bones, hear the word of the LORD! . . . I will make breath enter you, and you will come to life. . . . Then you will know that I am the LORD.' "

Ezekiel did as he was told. And the bones moved and came together.

Flesh appeared on them and breath entered them. They came to life and stood on their feet. Then the Lord said, "O my people, . . . I will put my Spirit in you and you will live, and I will settle you in your own land. Then you will know that I the LORD have spoken, and I have done it" (Ezek 37:1-14).

This expectation of a community renewed by the Spirit of the Lord, a community filled and governed by the living presence of God, flows out from Ezekiel into the future. Centuries later, the Christian church came to see itself as the fulfillment of Ezekiel's prophecy.

The Person of the Holy Spirit

Who is the Holy Spirit? Christians confess that he is "the third Person of the Trinity." They hold that the God revealed by Jesus Christ has three distinct ways of being God.

First, he is far beyond us. He is the mysterious Source of all things, visible and invisible. The greatness and the grandeur of his nature are reflected in his handiwork, the crashing waves on a New England shore, the predictability of the stars in their courses, the marvel of an infant's birth. He is beyond all that he has made. We call him Creator—and Father.

Second, God is before us. Jesus Christ demonstrated that God could veil himself in human flesh. He came to Bethlehem in the weakness of human birth. He submitted to the pains and frustrations of human life and died, at last, the vilest of human deaths. Yet through those thirty years, and especially through his resurrection from the dead, he succeeded in convincing his disciples that he was God. "God was in Christ," they preached. So he is before us. We call him Redeemer—the Son.

Third, God is within us. He is that life-giving Spirit who both witnesses to humanity about the truth of God and creates a unique community of twice-born people called the church. By the Holy Spirit, Jesus can be everywhere present today. He is no longer limited to the first century, to the Aramaic language, to the hills of Galilee and to a prescientific view of the world. The risen Christ is freed from the limits of time and space to walk into every person's life. By the Spirit he moves freely through the centuries and across cultures, making salvation available to all. We call that Presence the Holy Spirit.

How did Christians come to these convictions about the Spirit? They had the Old Testament Scriptures to guide them along a certain trail of thought, and they had the life and teachings of Jesus to point to the end of the trail—the Christian understanding of the life and ministry of the Holy Spirit.

The Spirit in the Old Testament

When the Old Testament speaks of *spirit,* it reflects one of the earliest ideas about human life, found in many parts of the ancient world: Human life is dependent upon breath. Even in sleep men and women continue to breathe. Doesn't the chest rise and fall? And when a man or woman dies, doesn't breath depart from the body? So breath means life.

Apparently reflecting this belief, the Old Testament word for spirit is *ruach,* which means breath, wind or spirit. So Genesis tells us how humankind was created: "The LORD God formed the man from the dust of the ground and breathed into his nostrils the breath of life, and the man became a living being" (Gen 2:7). God had his Spirit, and so did the man.

This fact raises an unavoidable question: What is the relation between human spirit and God's Spirit? Some Eastern religions teach that the human spirit is a tiny spark from the great fire of God, a beam from the cosmic light of God.

In the Old Testament, however, the spirit in men and women is never presented as some sort of fragment of the Spirit of God. Neither do the human spirit and God's Spirit share in some sort of cosmic life. People, like all other living things, are always dependent upon God for life. But unlike other creatures, the human spirit enables men and women to have a personal relationship with God. Men and women can know God and love God and serve God. The human spirit is special. It makes possible a free and conscious commitment to God; it offers men and women the possibility of personal contact with God.

Since the entrance of sin, however, men and women cannot know this relationship apart from God's special help. Sin turned the human freedom *for* God to a freedom *from* God. Human beings find it impossible to reverse this change. Only as the Spirit of God subdues the human spirit and makes people willing to confess their sin and their need of God's forgiveness do they know again the freedom for God.

This is the work of God's Spirit throughout the Old Testament. Time and again he comes upon men and women in order to advance the Lord's saving purpose. He is the hidden power behind Joseph's wisdom in Egypt, behind the skill of Bezalel in designing the tabernacle, behind the faithfulness of Caleb, behind the awe-inspiring feats of the judges and the inspiration of the prophets. In time the *ruach* of God comes to stand for the work of the righteous and merciful God of Israel. He is no pervasive force in the universe; he is the *invasive* power in Israel. The idea is not immanence, but action. The Spirit of God is the Lord God in working clothes.

In the latter parts of the Old Testament this active power of God is a sure sign of God's presence. God's presence and God's Spirit are essentially the same thing. That is why the psalmist prayed, "Do not cast me from your presence," and immediately followed with the parallel clause, "or take your Holy Spirit from me" (Ps 51:11).

When we reach the prophets, we feel a fresh breeze. Some of these seers—like Ezekiel—look beyond the invasion and ruin of Israel and see another day, a coming age when God will no longer give his Spirit only to judges, priests and prophets. He will pour out his Spirit upon everyone. As the prophet Joel put it: "Your sons and daughters will prophesy, your old men will dream dreams, your young men will see visions" (Joel 2:28).

In a similar way, Jeremiah promised a day when a new covenant of the Spirit would be written on the human heart. Men and women would no longer live under the promptings of the Law; they would have the inner direction of the Spirit of God.

This coming age of the Spirit, forecast by the prophets, centered in a Leader who would be able to say,

> The Spirit of the Sovereign LORD is on me,
>> because the LORD has anointed me
>> to preach good news to the poor.
> He has sent me to bind up the brokenhearted,
>> to proclaim freedom for the captives
>> and release from darkness for the prisoners. (Is 61:1)

The Old Testament, then, leaves us leaning forward, looking for a brighter day when the Spirit will move beyond Israel to liberate hosts of other people—even Gentiles—through the Anointed One, the Messiah.

Jesus and the Spirit

When a reader opens the New Testament, she is struck immediately by the fact that the Christian Gospels consider Jesus of Nazareth more than another prophet in Israel. The Spirit descended upon those ancient voices only now and then; in Jesus Christ, the Spirit of God lives in his fullness. The birth narratives in Matthew and Luke trace Jesus' conception to the power of the Spirit. These nativity scenes are apparently painted to show that Jesus' life was a direct creation of the Spirit.

So it naturally follows that when he opened his public ministry by his baptism at the hands of John the Baptist, the Spirit descended and, as John's Gospel says, "remained on him" (1:32). He received the Spirit "without limit." From that time on, the Spirit was united to Jesus. He had, as it were, no mission apart from Jesus.

That is apparently the meaning of Jesus' later invitation in the temple court: "If anyone is thirsty, let him come to me and drink. Whoever believes in me, as the Scripture has said, streams of living water will flow from within him." As the Gospel explains, he was speaking of the Spirit who would in time be given to all who believed. "Up to that time the Spirit had not been given, since Jesus had not yet been glorified" (Jn 7:37-39).

Time and again the Gospels trace Jesus' victories over hostile forces—demons, sickness and death—to the Spirit. That is why Jesus says, "If I drive out demons by the Spirit of God, then the kingdom of God has come upon you" (Mt 12:28). The Spirit of God, then, is the hidden explanation of Jesus' life.

Perhaps Peter gave the best summary when he explained, "God anointed Jesus of Nazareth with the Holy Spirit and power, and . . . he went around doing good and healing all who were under the power of the devil, because God was with him" (Acts 10:38).

In the New Testament, then, Jesus Christ is clearly the recipient and the bearer of the Holy Spirit. Men and women do not come to know the Spirit except through him.

But what about that great day of the Spirit that Ezekiel promised? When did those dry bones come together and take flesh and receive the breath of God? That came only after Jesus was "glorified"—after his death on Calvary and his resurrection from the grave. Christians call it Pentecost.

Pentecost

Pentecost was first a Jewish festival, coming seven weeks after Passover. Jesus' crucifixion took place during Passover, and at the next Pentecost excitement among the pilgrims in Jerusalem was running high. During the festival about 120 disciples of Jesus were meeting in a home when an unusual thing happened. Suddenly God's Spirit fell upon those gathered there. Some thought that it was a violent wind rushing through the house; others testified to tonguelike flames of fire resting on each of them.

Swept up in the experience, the disciples rushed into the streets and headed for the temple. Many of the visitors in the city saw them and followed because they heard their native languages coming from the lips of the disciples.

Once at the temple, Peter stood before the huge crowd and told them that the miracle they were witnessing was a fulfillment of the prophet Joel's promise about the outpouring of God's Spirit in the "last days." The explanation for the marvel, he said, lay in the recent crucifixion of Jesus of Nazareth. God had made him Lord and Messiah by raising him from the dead!

Peter's announcement of the resurrection was an astounding development. How could he ever substantiate such a claim? He appealed to the Jewish Scriptures, which said that the Messiah would not be abandoned in death but would be enthroned at God's right hand, the position of authority and honor, until universal victory was his (Ps 16:10; 110:1).

But what do such Scriptures have to do with Jesus of Nazareth? He was the Messiah, said Peter. We know it is so because "God raised this Jesus to life, and we are all witnesses of the fact" (Acts 2:32).

From the beginning, then, the apostles preached the resurrection of Jesus as the fulfillment of God's purpose announced in the Old Testament. Once crucified, the Messiah had been exalted above the universe. Apart from that miracle, said the apostles, there is no gospel, no salvation and no church. It is true. Therefore, "repent," Peter told the Pentecost pilgrims, "and be baptized . . . in the name of Jesus Christ for the forgiveness of your sins. And you will receive the gift of the Holy Spirit" (Acts 2:38).

The Mission of the Spirit

Since that moment the Spirit has been at work in the church bearing witness to Christ, making men and women alive to God, enlightening the minds of believers and changing them into the likeness of Christ. The Spirit's specific mission is to empower God's liberating forces launched by the appearance of Jesus Christ.

Through the Spirit the mission of Jesus assumed universal proportions. It spread from Palestine throughout the whole world, from the first century to all ages. The link between the historic appearance of Jesus and the universal ministry of the Holy Spirit is so close that the apostle Paul could say, "The Lord is the Spirit" (2 Cor 3:17).

We need not suppose that Paul intended an absolute identification between Christ and the Spirit. He still spoke of Christ as a person who once lived in Nazareth but now lives in the Hidden World. What he apparently intended was an identity of purpose between Christ and the

Spirit in their work of reconciliation. Both possess the same divine energy at work in Christian believers, renewing their inner life and leading them toward that day when even their spiritual bodies will reflect the glory and incorruptibility of Christ's resurrection body (Rom 8:11).

Today many people think of the Spirit of God as a kind of detached spiritual essence scattered throughout humanity, working here and there quite apart from Jesus Christ who redeemed us. That is not the view of the New Testament. The first Christians believed that the Holy Spirit comes to us from the Hidden World to reveal the Father Almighty, who through Jesus Christ delivers us from spiritual slavery and offers us life in a new dimension. They knew the Spirit not as an alternative to but as a manifestation of the presence of Christ.

The presence of the Spirit, then, does not displace the presence of Christ. That can never happen in the Christian faith. True faith must always center in Christ, through whom God reconciled the world to himself. It is the Holy Spirit who makes God personal to each of us by uniting us to Christ. He is that breath from God who makes our dry bones live.

12

WHISPERS OF THE WIND
THE SPIRIT'S WORK

According to the Gospel of John, Nicodemus, a member of the Jewish ruling council, came to Jesus one night and said to him, "Rabbi, we know you are a teacher who has come from God. For no one could perform the miraculous signs you are doing if God were not with him."

"I tell you the truth," said Jesus, "no one can see the kingdom of God unless he is born again."

Nicodemus hardly knew what to say. He had never heard of a second birth. "How," he asked, "can a man be born when he is old?"

"Flesh gives birth to flesh," Jesus explained, "but the Spirit gives birth to spirit. . . . The wind blows wherever it pleases. You hear its sound, but you cannot tell where it comes from or where it is going. So it is with everyone born of the Spirit" (Jn 3:1-8).

Christians have often wondered why Nicodemus, a respected religious leader, knew so little about the Holy Spirit. Apparently he had never heard of the new birth and wasn't sure what to make of Jesus. His problem is worth pursuing. What does the Spirit of God do in the world?

Jesus' comparison—the wind and the Spirit—is a helpful starting point. It contains a significant reminder: God's ways are not our ways. The Spirit's plans are not open and plain to all. Men and women can see the effects of his work, but no one can explain infallibly just how or where he moves. When people have dared to claim control over the Spirit of God, saying he is here or he is there, they have usually proved themselves fools.

> Oh, the depth of the riches of the wisdom and knowledge
>   of God!
> How unsearchable his judgments,
>   and his paths beyond tracing out! (Rom 11:33)

We dare to raise the question of the Spirit's work only because the Bible itself raises it and the Christian faith rests upon it. God, it seems, invites us to listen intently for the whispers of the Wind.

The Spirit in Creation

When Christians confess their faith in the Holy Spirit through the classic creeds, they refer to him as "the Lord and Giver of life." As we have seen, the link between the Spirit and the breath of life is basic. But what is life? One after another of the mysteries of the universe have yielded to the relentless investigations of the human mind. But this question remains unanswered. We can recognize life, and we can nurture life, and we can destroy life, but we cannot explain life.

The creeds' conviction that life comes from the Spirit can be traced to Jesus Christ, who once said to his disciples, "The Spirit gives life; the flesh counts for nothing" (Jn 6:63). What did Jesus mean? What life does the Spirit give? Is he the source of all natural life? Or is he the giver of eternal life to those who believe? Christians believe that he is both. Like a wind, he moves mysteriously through the natural world and through the spiritual realms.

The Bible portrays the Spirit as the energizing power in creation. "In the beginning," we read in the first verse of the Bible, "God created the heavens and the earth. Now the earth was formless and empty, darkness was over the surface of the deep, and the Spirit of God was hovering over the waters" (Gen 1:1-2).

The image of the hovering Spirit is a striking picture. It suggests a mother bird with outstretched wings, hovering over her young to cherish and protect them. The figure implies that the earth held the germs of life within it and that the Holy Spirit caused this life to spring forth in order that he might lead it to its intended destiny.

The Spirit of God appears a second time in the creation story, when the Lord God makes man "from the dust of the ground." He formed man and "breathed into his nostrils the breath of life, and the man became a living being" (Gen 2:7). The Hebrews apparently believed that the Spirit, this outgoing breath of God, was the source of life. Job, for example, said, "The Spirit of God has made me; the breath of the Almighty gives me life" (Job 33:4).

These references to the Spirit's activity in creation strongly suggest that he is present in the cosmic process at all levels, but in a special way in human life. Men and women can find their true life only as they fulfill their destiny. Human beings were created to have personal communion with God, and the Holy Spirit makes that possible. The apostle Paul reminded the Athenians of this when he told them, "The God who made the world and everything in it . . . gives all men life and breath and everything else" (Acts 17:24-25). This is the reason Christians hold that life itself is a sacred gift of God.

The Witness of the Spirit

What is the connection between the human spirit and the Holy Spirit? In the early days of Christianity, when the gospel spread beyond the limits of Judaism and entered the world of Greek culture, many Christians accepted the idea that the human spirit reflects in a special way the Holy Spirit. Irenaeus, the pastor of the church at Lyons, for example, argued, "The Word bestows the Spirit on all . . . on some by way of creation . . . ; on some by way of adoption." But this notion goes too far.

As Jesus suggested in his conversation with Nicodemus, sin has distorted the harmony that once existed between "flesh"—the natural person—and "Spirit"—the life of God. No natural communion is now possible between "flesh" and "Spirit." Men and women must be made alive by the Spirit if they are to "see the kingdom of God."

The original "likeness" to God's Spirit in the human spirit is not totally lost, however; some hint of the created purpose remains in human beings. This helps to explain humanity's sense of right and wrong. People everywhere, except the pathological, seem to feel guilty when they transgress some standard of morality. Specific sins seem to vary from culture to culture, but no tribe or society endures with total lawlessness. This conscience, as we call it, may be a clue to the life from the Spirit.

Christians have also traced humanity's love of the truth, displays of creativity and acts of generosity to the Spirit of God. Like James, they hold that "every good and perfect gift is from above, coming down from the Father of the heavenly lights, who does not change like shifting shadows" (Jas 1:17). In this sense, the scientist, the painter and the humanitarian are working with God as they make truth and beauty and goodness their goal. Christian theologians call this "common grace." They mean that the gifts of God are not limited to Christian people, but come through all people.

Perhaps, however, the supreme instance of the Spirit's ministry to all humankind is the religious quest that is almost universal. Over the centuries and throughout the world, men and women have tried to get into touch with the universal and the eternal. Men and women are compulsive worshipers. This spiritual longing is a human distinctive; it sets us off from all other creatures. Human beings seem to be permanently maladjusted to their environment, always searching for the Hidden World. Why? Christians believe that the restlessness at the center of human existence is a faint whisper of the Holy Spirit, inviting men and women to find life in Christ.

Since the appearance of God in flesh, the Holy Spirit often confronts men and women directly, on the basis of the apostolic witness to the Incarnation. He impresses them with their need to change, to be different people. That is his specific mission in preparation for a presentation of the gospel.

This is the mission Jesus stressed as he was leaving his disciples. "It is for your good that I am going away," he told them. "Unless I go away, the Counselor will not come to you; but if I go, I will send him to you. When he comes, he will convict the world of guilt in regard to sin and righteousness and judgment" (Jn 16:7-8). He proves men and women wrong in their ideas of a "benevolent" God who tolerates sin; wrong in their conceptions of righteousness, which suppose that they can achieve it apart from Christ; wrong in their impressions of judgment, which ignore the decisive place of the cross in God's eyes. All this is the Spirit's mission in the world.

The title Jesus gave the Spirit—"the Counselor"—is the Greek word *paraclete*—literally, the one who stands alongside. It is a title early Christians also used of Christ himself. He has come to stand by the believer's side, to speak in his defense, to uphold her when her knees begin to buckle. It is a vivid image of Jesus' work for us. But it is also his image of the Spirit's work. He is the other Counselor, the Voice at our side speaking of Christ.

In Washington, D.C., the Speaker of the House of Representatives has a parliamentary assistant who stands by constantly. The assistant anticipates the business of the House, the decisions to be made and the procedures to be followed. This person is always ready to give counsel and direction. The Speaker's representative is the *paraclete,* the one who stands by—an apt image of the Holy Spirit.

The Spirit in the Church

We might approach the second area of the Spirit's ministry through a picture drawn from today's urban world. The loneliness and isolation in contemporary urban societies can be illustrated by a ride in an elevator in an apartment building. You know the people around you are your neighbors, but you have no idea who they are. You glance around quickly, trying not to stare at anyone. You see the other riders but you do not speak. You are crowded together for a few brief moments, but there is no community. Finally, as the doors open upon the seventh floor, you are freed from the silent embarrassment. This is a portrait of what sociologist David Riesman once called "the lonely crowd."

The second ministry of the Holy Spirit addresses that need. He has come to create Christian community. The New Testament term for it is *koinonia*. It is the "common life of Christ" shared by the whole church; it is the fellowship of the Spirit.

We can find a vivid description of this "common life" just after the biblical account of the Spirit's appearance at Pentecost. The book of Acts tells us that the earliest believers "devoted themselves to the apostles' teaching and to the fellowship, to the breaking of bread and to prayer. . . . All the believers were together and had everything in common. . . . They broke bread in their homes and ate together with glad and sincere hearts, praising God and enjoying the favor of all the people" (Acts 2:42-47).

At Pentecost a new and vital corporate life entered the stage of history, a new spiritual community based upon common beliefs, mutual trust and, above all, life in the Spirit. Jesus Christ made it possible, and the Holy Spirit made it work. The Spirit was so real to these first Christians that they considered him the invisible leader of their community.

For example, in their report to the scattered churches after one conference, the disciples explained that they reached their decision because it "seemed good to the Holy Spirit and to us" (Acts 15:28). This was more than empty religious prattle. They believed deeply in their unseen companion. The apostle Paul reflected the same awareness of the Spirit's presence in his prayer for the "fellowship of the Holy Spirit" (2 Cor 13:14).

This creation of a united spiritual community was the primary purpose in the Holy Spirit's descent on the day of Pentecost. The Lord led Israel out of slavery in Egypt, through the desert, to the foot of Mount Sinai to establish his covenant with them and constitute them "the people of God." Likewise, at Pentecost the Holy Spirit took the good news of Jesus' death and resurrection and created the new covenant; he formed the new "people of God."

This spiritual oneness is more than a creedal statement; it is the heart of Christian reality. Professor J. A. Findlay once suggested that in Jesus' parable of the Pharisee and the publican, the Pharisee was probably repeating the familiar Jewish prayer: "God, I thank you that I was not born a Gentile, but a Jew: not a slave, but a free man: not a woman, but a man." And, Findlay continued, when Paul wrote, "In Christ there is neither Jew nor Greek, slave nor free, male nor female" he was deliberately contradicting each phrase of the prayer that he had been taught to pray in his childhood. "Something," said Findlay, "had happened to a man who can do this."[1]

Regeneration

Just what does happen to a person who receives the new life of the Spirit? What is the Spirit's ministry to a Christian believer?

According to the New Testament, the work of God in the gospel includes the objective events of Jesus' life and the subjective gifts of the Spirit's mission. Both are essential for salvation. We have already considered Christ's reconciling work for spiritual rebels. Now it might prove helpful if we trace the outline of the Spirit's work in believers.

The initial work of the Spirit in the Christian is the new birth that Jesus revealed to Nicodemus. Theologians call it "regeneration." The apostle Paul once called it the "new creation." It is that work of the Spirit that transforms a spiritually lifeless person into a child of God. It is the personal experience of Ezekiel's resurrected dry bones. In this regeneration no one receives another ego. The transformed individual is the same person. All his or her basic parts remain intact—except that after the Spirit's work, the person is alive to God.

Perhaps the best illustration of the new birth is found in the orchard. The successful grafting of a shoot of a cultivated apple tree upon the stock of a wild tree results in choice fruit on the once wild tree. Without the graft, the wild tree is incapable of bearing fruit worth eating. But let the gardener graft this tiny shoot upon the wild stock, and in time luscious apples will swell on the branches. Somehow the little graft has the remarkable power to convert the sap and the vital forces into something good.

We are all wild trees incapable of acceptable fruit. The Holy Spirit, however, grafts into all who trust in Christ something that by nature they lack. Then good things happen.

Sanctification

The second ministry of the Spirit in the believer involves those good things. Theologians call this "sanctification." It is the Spirit's mysterious life transforming the Christian into the likeness of Christ, producing in him or her all those virtues that remind others of Jesus Christ. Paul once called them "the fruit of the Spirit." He had in mind such things as love, joy, peace, patience, kindness, goodness, faithfulness, gentleness and self-control (Gal 5:22-23). These are the signs of sanctification.

If a court of law required evidence that a man were cruel, a prosecuting attorney would only have to produce the man's battered wife or his abused daughter. The convincing evidence would lie in the external acts. Just so, the life arising from the Holy Spirit is evident when the ego is gone from the center of life, when the selfish possessiveness of a man or woman has been curbed and one's dominant thought is changed from "What do I get out of it?" to "What can I do for Christ and others?"

This life from the Spirit is unique. We cannot equate it with any form of law-keeping, but neither can the true Christian use the Spirit as an excuse for lawlessness.

Any identification of life in the Spirit with obedience to rules and regulations leads to a terrible perversion. Such a link suggests that the Christian faith is something external, something that can be found in actions alone. And that is simply untrue. Such an attitude is only a step away from considering faith a matter of bookkeeping.

The simplicity of such a view gives it a certain attractiveness. You open an account with God. On the credit side you enter all the good things you do: attend church regularly, contribute to worthy charities, raise your children to respect the law. There are, of course, entries on the other side of the ledger: the theft of office equipment, the unreported income on the tax form, the little affair on the business trip. The goal of this conception of religion is to total both sides of the account and have the credits exceed the debits.

The disastrous mistake in all this is the belief that a decent person can earn God's favor. All sorts of evils result from this perverted scheme: self-righteousness, contempt for others, spiritual blindness.

The only escape from it is through the Holy Spirit. He convinces us that we have our religion all wrong. The Christian faith does not consist of feverish attempts to earn God's favor by being good. It consists of humble acceptance of God's mercy arising from Christ's goodness. What we need more than anything else is God's forgiveness—and we can have it if we will wholeheartedly believe that Christ's death and resurrection removed every barrier to our reconciliation with God. This reversal in thinking, however, is so radical that men and women do not achieve it without the help of the Holy Spirit.

Even at the point of accepting the gospel lies another danger. No sooner do people reject the "bookkeeping" plan of salvation than they are confronted by an equally dangerous alternative. The promise of freedom from "bookkeeping" religion opens up the possibility of abuse of Christian freedom.

When told that they are free from the yoke of religious regulations, some people jump to the conclusion that they are free from any master at all. The apostle Paul discovered how often Christian converts exchange the bondage of self-righteousness for slavery to self-expression. And it was he who spoke of "the law of the Spirit of life" (Rom 8:2).

Life in the Spirit, he said, is more than a sense of release from the slavery to sin and death; it is also a new personal passion and inward power to please the One who frees us. That is the reality of the new birth that eluded Nicodemus before his significant conversation with Jesus.

13

GOD IN
THREE PERSONS
THE TRINITY

The maps of the early explorers of America always included vast unexplored territories. Courageous seafarers had touched the shorelines of the continent, and what they had touched was real. But their maps reveal that they knew almost nothing about the uncharted wilderness of the interior.

The same is true when Christians speak of the inner life of God. They know that God revealed something of himself in his covenant with Israel, in the life, death and resurrection of Jesus Christ, and in the surprising appearance of the Holy Spirit at Pentecost. This disclosure of God recorded in Scripture, like the continental shoreline, is real, but where does it lead? What does it suggest about the interior life of God? The doctrine of the Trinity is the church's attempt to trace something of that reality.

The Christian creeds, guided by the shoreline revealed in Scripture, help to plot the way to the life of God. But, as Christians have always acknowledged, so much terrain remains a mystery. The doctrine of the Trinity is so difficult to understand because no other teaching of the church carries us so deeply into the nature of God himself. It is like plunging into the impenetrable forests of an uncharted continent.

Christians, however, encouraged by the clues along the shoreline, do not fear the unknown. On the contrary, as they look to God, their first response is not dread but praise. That is why they sing with George W. Frazer:

> Father, Son, and Holy Spirit—
> Three in one! we give thee praise
> For the riches we inherit,
> Heart and voice to Thee we raise!
> We adore Thee! we adore Three!
> Thee we bless, thro' endless days!
> ("God, Our Father, We Adore Thee")

What, then, do Christians mean when they sing of "three in one"? While affirming their belief in one God, Christians confess that the one true God has revealed himself as Father, Son and Holy Spirit.

To many people such a statement is sheer nonsense. It is utter foolishness to say God is both one and three. And even Christians themselves are often hard pressed to explain what they mean when they sing of the "blessed Trinity." They often appeal to the mysteries of their faith and make no attempt to spell out what they mean by this central doctrine of their religion.

Neither response should surprise us. Since God is who he is, Christians will always have to live with the mystery of the Trinity. When we ask about life in the Hidden World, we are probing both the ultimate reality of the visible universe and the baffling depths of personal existence. Both astrophysicists and psychiatrists freely confess their wonder before the unknown in outer and inner space. In fact, every area of serious study has its frontiers of knowledge where the known meets the unknown. Why should the Christian faith apologize for its mysteries?

The Experience of the Trinity

So the first approach to the wonder of the holy Trinity is not in a naive question of mathematics: one or three? After all, Christians have never confessed God's unity and his plurality in the same sense. They came to faith in the holy Trinity not through mathematics but through revelation and experience. They could not testify of what God had done for them and to them in any way other than through the doctrine of the Trinity.

Israel's faith focused upon God the Creator of all things, the Lord of heaven and earth, who revealed himself to Israel by his great redeeming acts. He delivered the enslaved people of Israel from Egypt; he led them through their wilderness journey; he gave them a land of their own; he sent them prophets and kings. And through all these events Israel came to worship the Lord as a God of righteousness and grace. Even when the nation faced ruin, in the face of foreign invaders, a remnant in Israel saw that the Lord was somehow working out his purpose for his people.

This faith in a God who is the Father Almighty passed on to Christianity primarily because it was the faith Jesus taught and demonstrated to his disciples. The disciples saw, however, that Jesus was himself an inextricable part of that faith. When they tried to explain what Jesus meant to them, they found no adequate word except the word "Lord."

By identifying Jesus with Yahweh, the Lord of the Old Testament, early Christians knew full well what an incredible claim they were making. Yet they faced gladly the ridicule that followed the claim. They could not escape the impact of Jesus upon them and the compelling evidence they found of his deity, primarily his resurrection from the grave. He held the keys of death and hell. So to tell the truth about Jesus of Nazareth, they announced in Jerusalem that he was in fact God. The Lord had come to earth in human flesh.

The first Christians also said they experienced an indwelling Presence, a Power not their own. When he was with them, Jesus had promised to send to them—after his death and resurrection—his Spirit. And so it happened.

As we have seen, fifty days after Jesus' resurrection the disciples experienced in Jerusalem an overwhelming event—wind and fire and tongues! All who spoke of this supernatural power interpreted it to mean the fulfillment of Jesus' promise. His Spirit—and at the same time the Father's Spirit—had come to fill them and empower them to witness of God's work for them and in them.

This was more than an exalted spiritual or mystical mood of the soul. This was God's Spirit sweeping into the human spirit. It was the birth of the church, the community of God. The Lord of the exodus and Sinai, the same divine Person who gave the law and sent the Sacrifice, had come to create a new community of faith.

These three realities, then—the Father Almighty, the incarnate Word, the empowering Holy Spirit—were more than a mathematical riddle, more than a doctrine propounded by theologians. They were a single personal reality in the lives of Christians, a single relationship to the one God as Father, revealed in Christ and made real through the Spirit.

The first Christians professed this faith as they were baptized in the name of the Father, Son and Holy Spirit (Mt 28:17-21), and as they sought the benediction of heaven through "the grace of the Lord Jesus Christ, and the love of God, and the fellowship of the Holy Spirit" (2 Cor 13:14).

Plurality in unity is often a mark of creative genius. The *Unfinished Symphony* first existed in the mind of Schubert; it then became "incarnate" in a score written on paper and sounds produced by instruments; then it became a spirit, so that a music lover in New Zealand can write to a music lover in Sweden and ask—without any need to play the music for confirmation—how and why the third movement was never written.[1]

Anyone who tries to dismiss the Trinity as an antiquated theological riddle is dismissing the Christian God—and with him the Christian faith. This doctrine is the foundation of the Christian life. We cannot enter into the full meaning of God as he was revealed to the first Christians unless we enter into the meaning of the God who is revealed as Father, Son and Holy Spirit.

Across the centuries, Christians have claimed that God as Holy

Trinity fits their own actual experience of God. Take prayer. The Christian believer comes to God the Father. That is the characteristic movement of prayer. But he comes to God "through Jesus Christ our Lord." Christ is not only God's means of approaching us; he is also our door of access to the Father. Finally, if Christians pray at all, they pray "in the Spirit." The life from God that enables the Christian to come to God is the Holy Spirit. Father, Son and Spirit, then, are realities of the life of prayer, yet we know that it is the one God we meet in the experience of prayer.

The Doctrine of the Trinity

For a century or so after the ministry of Jesus, Christians did not put their new experience of God into explanatory words. As Leonard Hodgson, the Oxford theologian, once put it, Christianity was a trinitarian religion before it had a trinitarian theology.[2] The doctrine of the Trinity was the theology required by the trinitarian faith. The earliest Christians, like the Jews before them, intended to remain strict monotheists, but they also worshiped Jesus and exulted in the presence of the Holy Spirit—just as men and women through the ages enjoyed light without ever bothering to explain it.

Even the earliest trinitarian expressions of the Christian faith prevented Christianity from falling under the influence of either pantheistic or deistic religions. A faith in God which is at the same time faith in Jesus Christ as Lord can never be pantheistic, because Jesus Christ claimed to be the exclusive truth and life of God. He revealed God to humankind at a particular time through a particular life. In a similar way, a faith in God which is also a faith in the Holy Spirit cannot become deistic, because through the Holy Spirit Almighty God acts directly, and at times miraculously, in human affairs.

When the early Christians first tried to explain their trinitarian faith in terms that outsiders could understand, they often resorted to two basic explanations. These two different tracks reached the same fundamental point: the absolute unity and uniqueness of God. We call one "subordinationism" and the other "monarchianism." Both proved to have major weaknesses as enduring explanations of trinitarian reality, but both moved the church toward greater clarity in its faith.

Subordinationism

Greek religious philosophy often explained reality in terms of a supreme Mind—a transcendent First Principle. Under this sovereign Ruler there was a hierarchy of divine beings that acted as intermediaries between the supreme Mind and the physical world. These divine beings served as a cosmic ladder extending from the changeless realm to the material universe. Divinity was a matter of degree. Thus, one could speak of a plurality of divine beings while retaining an ultimate unity in reality.

In such a setting it was tempting for Christians to describe the Trinity by appealing to these Greek ideas of a supreme Power and his subordinate divine beings. But this temptation was dangerous. It suggested that when the New Testament spoke of "Father, Son and Holy Spirit" it meant "the ultimate God and two intermediaries." Why should the God of the Bible, the God of creation and Sinai and Calvary, need intermediaries? Is he somehow banned from his own creation?

Furthermore, what can we mean if we say Jesus Christ is divine but at the same time say that he is not in the fullest sense God? Are we to believe that Jesus Christ, worshiped as Lord ever since his resurrection, was only some envoy of the true God? Clearly, subordinationism wanted to avoid any hint of three gods (tritheism), but in adopting the traditional Greek idea of intermediaries it had introduced another set of unacceptable ideas about the Trinity.

The most troubling case for subordinationism came from a popular minister in Alexandria, Egypt, early in the fourth century. Arius felt that his bishop had distorted the unity of God. To set the record straight, Arius started preaching about the differences between the Father and the divine Logos (the Word). He turned to the Greek idea of the God beyond existence, who is the one source of all things.

Arius interpreted the Word, who assumed flesh, as a creature different in essence from God the Father. He is unlike any other creature;

he is "before times and before ages." He is divine and unique. And yet "there was a time when he was not." He does not share God the Father's uncreated existence.

Arius apparently had a knack for public relations and encouraged his followers to turn out catchy jingles and set his doctrine to bawdy tunes for barbershop harmony.

> If you want the Logos-doctrine,
> I can serve it hot and hot—
> God begot him and before he was begotten,
> he was not.

Before this distortion of the Holy Trinity could be suppressed, the emperor, Constantine, had to convene a general council of the church. Hundreds of church leaders had to debate the pros and cons for two generations.

Monarchianism

The sharp alternative to subordinationism in the early church was monarchianism. The name comes from the attempt to retain a faith in one holy Monarch of all creation. Christians who attempted to explain the Trinity in this way saw the weaknesses of subordinationism. So they asked, why not dispense with any real distinctions in the Trinity? Why not say that the Trinity is the one indivisible God?

When asked to explain the expression "Father, Son and Holy Spirit," the monarchists responded that these titles are merely different ways in which God is seen by human beings. They may be different designations of his attributes, much as the sun is bright and hot and round, or they may be three appearances of the one God—first as Father, then as Son and now as Spirit. But in either case, they do not refer to any essential distinctions within the supreme Monarch.

Three in One

Perceptive Christians, however, saw that this view of God was seriously deficient in describing the revelation of God recorded in the Bible. The designations Father, Son and Holy Spirit do in fact refer to something real within God.

To identify these distinctions, the church used the Greek term *hypostases* and its Latin counterpart *personae*. Our English word *persons* comes from the Latin. Whether in Greek or in Latin, the early Christians intended to designate something genuinely threefold when they spoke of Father, Son and Holy Spirit. They knew that the Trinity is more than three attributes or three appearances of God. Within his own mysterious being God *is* Father, Son and Holy Spirit. The designations are just ways in which God is God. Within the Godhead there are three "persons" who are neither three Gods nor three parts, but coequally and coeternally God.

The trouble with our English word *person* is its connotation of "personality." It carries the idea of an individual center of conscious life and independent activity. So "three persons" suggests to us Tom, Dick and Harry. Such an idea is obviously inappropriate in regard to God. But the early Christians, who spoke either Greek or Latin, never intended these ideas when they spoke of God "in three persons."

What early Christians wanted to affirm were the actual distinctions within the Godhead—the bearers of the differing relations within the one Almighty God. *Person,* applied to God, meant a genuine and self-supported presentation of the reality of God.

While Christians knew that the names Father, Son or Logos, and Spirit were analogies of God's inherent life, they believed that the names corresponded to what God was really like. Some actual distinctiveness was behind the titles Father, Son and Spirit. And that distinctiveness was not three gods, but a trinity within the one personal God.

In summary, the Father is God, the Son is God and the Spirit is God. The result is not three gods, but one. What they share equally and completely is deity. At the same time, the Father is not the Son, the Son is not the Spirit and the Spirit is not the Father. The distinctions are real. The "Persons," then, are within the one personal deity.

Beyond that summation, perhaps the best Christian response is praise in song—precisely what we find in the churches. After all, genuine love always moves beyond descriptions to the wonder of reality.

14
NEW PEOPLE
THE CHURCH

The organized church doesn't have much to offer me anymore," said one thoughtful critic. "In my opinion, the institutional conglomerate we call the church today is not the church that was ordained by God. . . . It seems the modern church in America long ago cut its ties to that God-ordained foundation and has been drifting with the cultural current ever since."[1]

To support his charge Mike Yaconelli pointed to the churches' costly buildings, their professional leaders and their ingrown meetings. He was too close to the truth to make any conscientious Christian comfortable.

The charges are real. The church is always in danger of losing itself in that surrounding society that the New Testament calls "the world"—human life organized and functioning without any thought of God. The process is subtle and slow. First, the church begins to admire the world. Next, it tries to appeal to the world. Then it adopts the standards and methods of the world. In the end the church has nothing to bring to the world because they are so much alike. That is why everything that goes by the name cannot justly be called "the church."

Organization and Organism

What is the church? Is it an earthly institution often in danger of deadly compromise with secular culture? Or is it a living spiritual organism nurtured by the life from God?

It is, in a sense, *both* organization and organism. Like Jesus, it is both earthly and heavenly. It is in the world without drawing its life from human sources. It is an organization in time and an organism in touch with eternity. It has a mission to the human race and a life from God. That is how the church exists: stretched in the tension between structure and spirit.

In one sense, the church is an institution, like other human institutions. It has boundaries that set it off from other agencies in society. It has a history that can be studied. It has ceremonies to observe at special times and designated places for its worship. In short, the church cannot escape history; it can fulfill its mission only as an organization.

Some Christians do not want to accept that fact. They try to release the church from time and space. They want to deliver the true people of God from the embarrassment of officials and property and customs.

But all such attempts prove unsuccessful in the end. To free Christianity from history and culture, one must make it a philosophy of noble ideals. But the gospel has never been good advice; it is good news. God acted in time; and he still does. That is why the church is in one sense an institution. It lives and serves in time.

In another sense, however, the church is a spiritual organism, a living body in society. Although it consists of men and women, it is impelled by the purpose of God and sustained by the presence of God. This relation to God determines the nature and mission of the church. It is the community that God gathers, the worship that he inspires, the mission that he sends. That mission is to enlist a people loyal to Jesus Christ, empower them by the new life of the Spirit and send them back into the world to witness and to care in Jesus' name.

At the heart of the Bible's description of the church is the idea of call. It is cradled in the term most often used to designate the church. The Greek term *ekklēsia* is built upon the root of the verb meaning "to call." The *ekklēsia* is the assembly or community called together by God.[2]

The Call of God

The church, as the Bible describes it, is more than an aggregation— people who have chosen to come together. It is a congregation, a people called together by the Word of God, the gospel of Christ's love and forgiveness. God comes first, then the church. His call to salvation precedes the gathering of the people. As Paul puts it, we are called into "fellowship with [God's] Son" (1 Cor 1:9).

What, then, is this life to which the church is called? What is God's purpose for his people in the world?

The New Testament makes clear that the church is the primary consequence of the redemptive acts of God in Christ. God sent Jesus as the Savior of men and women. That is the meaning of his name: the Lord is Savior. And as we have seen, he accomplished his mission magnificently. By his death on the cross and his resurrection from the grave, he removed every barrier to the presence of God. He opened the gates to the Hidden World.

Confirmation of Jesus' success came with the miraculous descent of the Holy Spirit at Pentecost. The Spirit came not only to confirm the merit of the Sacrifice but, just as important, to create a new people of God. All that Jesus secured for the people of God, the Spirit came to deliver. "I am come," Jesus once said, "that they might have life" (Jn 10:10 KJV). He obtained it and the Holy Spirit delivered it. Those who receive it are the people of God, the church of the living God.

Scriptures use a number of images to describe the nature and mission of the church. But three of the most common images highlight the church's special relationship with the Holy Trinity: Father, Son and Holy Spirit. Peter, for example, writing to "God's elect" throughout Asia Minor (today's Turkey), reminds them that they are "chosen according to the foreknowledge of God the Father, through the sanctifying work of the Spirit, for obedience to Jesus Christ and sprinkling by his blood" (1 Pet 1:2). The Father chooses the church, the Spirit sanctifies it and the Son atones for it.

This line of thought leads to three of the most widely used images of the church in Christian writings: the family of God, the body of Christ and the temple of the Spirit.

The Family of God

The idea of the family of God is implicit in the prayer Jesus taught his disciples to pray (Mt 6:9-13; Lk 11:1-4). When you pray, he said, say, "our Father." The sense of family is there. We do not pray, "my Father"; we pray, "our Father."

This life in God's family suggests a special relationship to God. Within the church God is no longer some impersonal Power in the universe, some invisible, ill-defined fear that clouds the future. No! He is the one Jesus taught us to call "heavenly Father."

The apostle Paul recognized the same relationship when he reminded the Ephesian Christians that in God's eyes they were no longer foreigners and aliens. They were "members of God's household" (Eph 2:19).

The church addresses a deep-seated need in the human heart— the need to belong, to be a part of a significant community. The hosts of human organizations testify to this need. Clubs, gangs, tribes, lodges, unions, fraternities—the list is almost endless.

Human beings, it seems, are made to belong. What, after all, is the most excruciating punishment in penal institutions? Solitary confinement. Why? Because loneliness is hell. God created human beings for loving fellowship, and the marred image of God in men and women witnesses to this thirst that cannot be quenched. The gospel is God's invitation to come to Christ and drink. Those who do come find that fellowship in the family of God.

This portrait of the church as God's family assumes unusual tones in the light of the idea of "the new covenant." The term *covenant* has almost dropped from our vocabulary, but in biblical times covenants were as common as contracts in our day. They were the acceptable way of establishing relationships. A covenant bound friend to friend (1 Sam 18:3) or established water rights between two tribal leaders (Gen 21:22-32) or expressed the terms of peace between two kings (1 Kings 20:34). It was a ready concept, therefore, to express the relation between God and his people.

In both instances—the old covenant between the Lord and Israel and the new covenant between the Lord and the church—God prepared his people to accept the covenant by a dramatic act. He brought his people to the solemn assembly at Mount Sinai by miraculously delivering them from the hands of the Egyptians. There, after pointing to their exodus from Egypt, God said to Israel, "I bore you on eagles' wings and brought you to myself" (Ex 19:4 RSV). The heart of the old covenant, then, was this special relationship between the Lord and his people.

The new covenant between God and the church was established by the death and resurrection of Jesus. On the night of his betrayal, Jesus told his disciples that his death, depicted by the cup of his last supper with them, was "the new covenant in my blood" (Lk 22:20). Unlike the old covenant expressed in laws written on stone, this covenant was etched by the Spirit on the hearts and consciences of Christian believers, just as the prophets had predicted it would be.

It is important to stress that this covenant with God was not a bargain that human beings struck with the Almighty. Pagan religions were filled with such ideas of covenants. Their devotees were desperately trying somehow to please the gods in order to enter into an agreement and escape their wrath.

In striking contrast, Israel's covenant was not one they offered to God. On the contrary, God took the initiative; by delivering Israel from Egyptian slavery, he graciously presented the covenant to them. Similarly, in the cross and resurrection of Jesus, God offers himself to believers freely. His grace, his surprising love and his forgiveness are extended to his people long before they turn and receive his mercy.

The recognition of this grace of God in the covenant inspires the church to sing with Samuel Davies,

> O may this strange, this matchless grace,
> This Godlike miracle of love,
> Fill the whole earth with grateful praise,
> And all th' angelic choirs above.
> Who is a pard'ning God like Thee?
> Or who has grace so rich and free? ("Great God of Wonders")

The Body of Christ

The second biblical image of the church is the body of Christ. The meaning of the expression is not self-evident. In recent years many Christians have mistakenly taken the phrase to mean "the body of Christians," a collection of individual believers. The church obviously includes people, but the Bible does not say "the body of Christians." It says "the body of Christ." Christians are members of the body; they represent the diversity. The body is Christ's; he creates the unity.

Another possible understanding of the expression is "the community that belongs to Christ." This view takes "of Christ" as a possessive and therefore sets the church off from other bodies. Such a view, however, leaves Christ aside, much as an owner of a horse is something totally different from the animal itself.

While it is true, in one sense, that the church belongs to Christ—he "purchased" it with his blood (Rev 5:9)—the idea the apostle seems to have in mind when he speaks of "the body of Christ" is the intimate union of Christ with his people and the life-giving energy he provides for them.

Interestingly, the apostle Paul never calls the church "the torso of Christ," with the head as something different and presumably separable from the torso. No, *body* is an inclusive term, designating the torso, with its various parts, *and* the head. We should not think of the church, then, as something apart from Christ. The church is the body of Christ only when he is present and included.

Certainly Jesus is more than another founder of a religion. By his death and resurrection he does more than establish the church; he constitutes it. He gives it reality. Like the head of any body, he directs the actions of the church. And like digested food, he energizes the body as its life-giving power. Through this body, Christ continues his work of salvation in the world.

The Temple of the Spirit

The third figure the apostles use to describe the church is the building, the temple of the Spirit. Both Peter and Paul adopt the image. Peter, for example, in his first letter to "God's elect" in Asia Minor says, "You also, like living stones, are being built into a spiritual house to be a holy priesthood, offering spiritual sacrifices acceptable to God through Jesus Christ" (1 Pet 2:5).

The metaphor is obviously mixed. The church is both the building, growing by the addition of each living stone (believer), and the priesthood that offers sacrifices of praise to God in the temple.

Peter's intention, however, is clear enough. The church, in his image, is the spiritual fulfillment of the whole temple experience maintained in Israel for centuries. God, who once appeared in the holy place in Jerusalem, now lives in the church by his Spirit. And the cornerstone of the building—the piece that determines the purpose of every other living stone—is Jesus Christ. He is the determining One. Either men and women find God's purpose for them and are added to this spiritual temple under construction, or else they stumble in unbelief over the Cornerstone, Jesus Christ, and are crushed.

In Christianity, then, religion acceptable to God is not dependent upon holy rites conducted in sacred buildings. God's temple is the church. He comes to men and women who come to him through the great High Priest and are added to his temple by being aligned with the Cornerstone. God's chosen sanctuary is his people.

Within this spiritual temple, all who are joined to Jesus Christ by faith share in the priesthood. In contrast to Judaism, in which only members of a single tribe functioned as priests, Christianity knows no special priesthood. All who come to God by faith in Christ share in the service of the sanctuary. What was unthinkable in Judaism is fundamental in Christianity. Proselytes become priests! The whole community of faith offers sacrifice.

The sacrifices are no longer animals slain in prescribed ceremonies. They are spiritual and moral. The sacrifices of the church are obedience to God, the praises of God, a contrite spirit and practical service to needy people. This worship and service is pleasing to God because it is brought through Jesus Christ.

These images of the church reveal the significant ways that Christianity broke through the restrictive institutions of Judaism and emerged as a universal faith. A distinctive priesthood serving in a distinctive temple for a distinctive people with a distinctive tradition was now a thing of the past. The church had no special priesthood, no special building in a special place. The gospel is for all peoples in all places. Faith in Christ introduces a believer immediately into a universal confessional community which spans time and place.

It is precisely because the church is for all people that it can find embodiment in every place. Believers are drawn by the Spirit to meet with those living in the same vicinity who profess this same faith-loyalty to Jesus Christ. This is why the New Testament writers speak of the church (ekklēsia) in either of these senses. It is the universal body of all who profess faith in Jesus Christ as Savior and Lord. But at the same time it is the local assembly of those in a given place who make that profession.

The New Testament never suggests a conflict between the universal confessional community and the local gathered community. Apparently the apostles thought of only one church, because there is only one Savior and Lord of the church. In the Bible the church is not defined in terms of how many people make it up, but in terms of the distinctive life of God within the community.

Think of binoculars. As you look through the eyepieces, a bird is greatly magnified. But if you turn the binoculars around and look at the goldfinch through the lens end, it is greatly reduced. In all respects except size it is the same bird. So with the church.

In the day-to-day life of the Christian it is important that the church have a tangible presence. For each person it must appear in a particular place and at a particular time—for example, the First Presbyterian Church of Springfield, Idaho, in 1995. Such a concrete expression of the church makes the community of faith a living reality. It is no mere abstraction. It is here and now, pointing to the presence of the people of God. And in the local church the people of God have faces.

Some Christians have tried to equate the universal church and the kingdom of God. That has often proved to be a foolhardy move. Such an equation tends to encourage the church to grasp for earthly power and to abuse it. The Bible indicates that the kingdom of God is God's rule and reign. The church is only the sphere where this has begun. British theologian P. T. Forsyth once called the church "the kingdom in the making."

At the same time the church is the herald of the kingdom. By announcing the good news of Christ's appearing and the forgiveness available to men and women, it is inviting people to surrender to the reign of Christ. The lordship, however, is always Christ's.

We also need to draw a clear distinction between the church and the state. In the Christian view of God's will in the world, the state is not simply a product of human design. It is a providential means of protecting society from the destructive forces of human nature and fostering civility in public life. Some theologians call this the "strange work of Christ": even among those who do not profess to follow Christ, he works invisibly to achieve civil order. As the apostle Paul put it, "There is no authority except that which God has established" (Rom 13:1).

In that sense, the church and the state complement each other. They both strive for human well-being, but their means differ. The state relies on might and coercion. The church depends upon the vigorous announcement of the truth, and the visible demonstration of it in the world.

With these images and distinctions in mind, we can now return to our original question. When Christians confess their faith "in the holy catholic church," as they have done since the early third century, what do they have in mind? Some institution? What is the point of confessing faith in an institution? The point is that Christians have always believed the church is more than an institution. It is the family of God, the body of Christ and the spiritual temple of the Spirit.

Faith in the church in this sense acknowledges that we cannot live the Christian life in isolation, like some religious Robinson Crusoe. Membership in the church is not an optional extra. The fact is, we cannot be fully Christian without belonging to the church. As we study the New Testament we find that to be a Christian is to be "in Christ," and that this means being a member of the new society of which Christ is the living Head—the church. The New Testament knows nothing of unattached Christians.

Consider the matter in a more mundane way. What would we think of a man who said that he wanted to be a soldier but insisted that he could be a perfectly good one without joining the army? An unattached soldier is nonsense—and so is the notion of a solitary Christian.

In short, membership in the church, far from being a matter of personal choice, is a spiritual necessity. All true Christian experience is ecclesiastical experience—experience gained, enriched and matured in the presence of Christ and his people.

15
THE BASIC STEPS
GRACE

The early-twentieth-century American evangelist Billy Sunday once said, "Going to church don't make a man a Christian any more than going to a stable makes a man a horse."

Many people questioned Sunday's style, but no one missed his point. It is possible to trust in a religious institution which cannot save in order to hide from the only God who can. But if the purpose of the church is not to make us Christians, what is it?

As we have seen, when Christians confess their belief in the church, as they have done through the Christian centuries, they have in mind something more than another human institution. Belief in the church means faith in the life of God found in the church.

It is always possible to see the outward behavior of the church—its worship services or its impact on society—and to dismiss it as another "thing"—a place to go, perhaps, or a program to operate. Such views are reflected in our conversation. We speak of "going to church" or "directing the program." Both suggest that the church is under human control.

But the church is not really a "thing." The moment you think of it as a "thing" you go astray. You cannot leave God out of the picture. The church is God's people. By his Spirit he lives within the community, shaping its life and character. That means the purpose of the church is to honor God's name and to serve his cause.

The church experiences the life of God in two fundamental ways: in the gathering and in the scattering of the people of God—in worship and in service. The first is for the growth of the body in the love of God; the second is for the work of the body for the needs of people. One is the inward journey of faith; the other is the outward journey of faith. Either way, in a secular society it is always possible for the church to miss the purpose of God.

The Gathered Church

The church is often tempted to turn its gathering into a distortion of God's purpose. It is easy to think of God's grace, his gift of transforming love, as a commodity, and to picture the church as a religious establishment for the distribution of goods and services to the community. God has stocked the shelves with religious merchandise such as worship, counseling, fellowship and instruction. In this arrangement, church leaders serve as the proprietors of the retail outlet. They direct the distribution of spiritual services to the customers.

This institutional view of the church prides itself in the legality of the franchise, the quality of its goods and the authority of its proprietors. It measures success in terms of satisfied customers, so the church becomes a business—God's business.

But the church can veer just as quickly from God's purpose as it scatters throughout a city. If the church is primarily a social movement supporting all the right causes, it is easy to think of it as a civil demonstration, a group of people marching together for a common goal: the improvement of human life on earth. Unlike the institution that emphasizes its authorization and its goods, the demonstration measures its success in terms of social benefits—fair housing, for example, or women's rights.

The demonstration image can also allow the secular world to intrude. It can subvert the purpose of God by making the humanitarian impulse basic. The needs of men and women can undercut the purposes of God.

The Ministry of the Word

The only corrective for these perversions is a clear vision of the church under the Word of God. The community of faith obedient to the Lord's purpose must maintain a balance between gathering for the renewal of the life of God in the body and scattering for the ministry of the Word of God in the world. In both cases the Word of God is the essential element.

"The Word," said Martin Luther, "is the one perpetual and infallible mark of the Church." When the church gathers, what it hears must be the Word of God; when the church scatters, what it shares must be the Word of God.

The Word of God is a biblical expression, but its meaning is not self-evident. What do we mean by the Word of God? Basically, it means anything God does or says to communicate himself to humanity. It is God actively making himself known to us.

The supreme way God has done this is the Incarnation—Jesus Christ, God's living Word. God broke through the invisibility of the Hidden World and communicated himself to us by sending his Son. Christians call him Immanuel, meaning "God with us."

Scripture and Sacrament

How does God communicate the Word to people today?[1] He does it in three ways:

First, through the Scriptures, the Word of God written. The church describes these writings as the Word of God because in them God makes himself known as Creator and Redeemer. Christians may tell the story of God's redeeming work in such a way that the story itself becomes an act of God in the lives of those who hear it and take its message personally.

Second, through the gospel, the spoken Word of God. The Bible must be accepted as the truth and communicated by those who understand it. It must be set forth in living thought and speech. "Faith," said the apostle, "cometh by hearing, and hearing by the Word of God" (Rom 10:17 KJV). So it is not the Bible as a dead book but the message of the Bible understood, accepted and proclaimed that is the medium of the Spirit of God in the church. It is the Spirit and the Word. The Spirit is the courier of God; the Word is his communiqué.

The church has used a host of means to communicate this message of God. In the gathered community, however, it has most often used music, Scripture reading, creeds, testimony, art and, above all, preaching to relate the Word of God to contemporary believers. Preaching links the first-century events recorded in the Bible to the life of men and women today. It applies the timeless truth of God to human tragedies and celebrations, death and birth, depression and elation. That is why the Word of God preached is a constituting element in the continuing life of the church.

Third, through the sacraments, the Word of God enacted. Christians have always held that two ritual observances, instituted by Jesus Christ himself, are vital elements in the worship of the people of God. These are baptism and the Lord's Supper. Some Christians consider them important symbols of the grace of God received through faith in Jesus; other Christians assert that the two rituals actually confer the spiritual life that they picture. In both cases, Christians maintain that the ceremonies are for perpetual observance in the church. Most Christians call them *sacraments*. Many others prefer the word *ordinances*.

To the secular-minded person these two ceremonies probably appear silly: a gathering of otherwise sensible adults to watch as a friend is plunged under water, or a gathering around a table to eat bits of dried bread and take sips of diluted wine. What is this all about?

The term *sacrament* comes from a Latin word, *sacramentum*. This word originally referred to the Roman soldier's oath of allegiance to his emperor. When the Christians took over the term, they thought of those ceremonies that bound them in loyalty to Christ, the Captain of their salvation. The term *ordinance* stresses the same basic idea of Christ's authority. It reminds us that Jesus "ordained" these two ceremonies for perpetual observance.

The sacraments, then, are visible signs of a spiritual reality, Christ's encounter with his people. In the sacraments the word of forgiveness and grace is depicted within the church. They are enacted sermons. They appeal to our souls through our senses, and, by the witness of the Holy Spirit, they make the Savior real to his people.

Baptism

The first sacrament (or ordinance) is baptism, the rite by which a believer is inducted into the fellowship of the church. That has been the Christian practice ever since the days of the apostles.

The idea apparently came from Jesus. He accepted baptism at the hands of his cousin John the Baptist, whose preaching linked the outward ceremony with inward repentance. Jesus endorsed the same practice and urged his disciples to make other disciples and baptize them in the name of the Father, Son and Holy Spirit. By this command he related baptism to the total saving work of the Trinity and prescribed it as the universal practice of the church.

The apostle Paul gave the early churches the most extensive theological explanation of baptism. He spelled out its significance in terms of death and resurrection. He told the Roman believers that retributive justice cannot be executed upon a dead man. Just so Christians, united by faith to the death of Christ, are free from the condemnation of sin, and through the resurrection of Christ they share a totally new life. Baptism is the depiction of this spiritually transforming experience.

Over the centuries Christians have debated what baptism accomplishes, to whom it should be administered and how much water should be used. The New Testament itself seems to emphasize the central importance of faith for baptism. It is administered to those who stand humbly before God in the grace and mercy of God revealed in the death and resurrection of Jesus.

At the moment of baptism the Christian makes an irrevocable commitment to Christ, whose death provides forgiveness and whose life from the dead makes possible the power to live by faith. By this confession of faith in baptism, men and women enter a new relationship with God and are added to the fellowship of the Spirit in the life of the church.

By accepting baptism, Christians devote themselves to spiritual growth and to the standards of the fellowship into which they have been inducted. Baptism, then, is more than a religious ceremony; it is a moral and spiritual pledge of devotion to Christ and to his people.

The Lord's Supper

The second sacrament is the memorial meal instituted by Jesus on the eve of his death on the cross. As he celebrated the Jewish Passover with his disciples, he gave them bread to eat and wine to drink and said, "This is my body given for you. . . . This cup is the new covenant in my blood, which is poured out for you" (Lk 22:19-20; see also Mt 26:26-28; Mk 14:22-24). Since that hour the ceremony has served as the focal point of Christian worship.

Christians have differing names for the sacred meal. Some, recalling its institution by Christ, call it the Lord's Supper. Others call it Holy Communion, as a reminder of the fellowship of believers with their Lord and with other believers. Some call it the Eucharist, which means thanksgiving; these want to stress that the people of God receive the bread and the cup with grateful joy. Under whatever name, however, Christians see the reminder of the gospel and the forgiveness of sin that is available to the believer.

The primary significance of the Lord's Supper is the representation of Christ's death as the basis of the new covenant between God and his people. The breaking of Christ's body and the shedding of his blood were the sacrifice necessary to reconcile men and women to God.

In the sacred meal bread and wine enter and are assimilated into our physical bodies to contribute to our life and health—a dramatic picture of the life of Christ entering spiritually into the life of the grateful believer. Thus, the Lord's Supper constantly renews the saving power of Christ for the believing community and each member of it.

By instituting this meal for perpetual observance, Jesus apparently intended to keep alive for his disciples the memory of his purpose. They were to serve him until he returned to them. He gave few details of their mission, but he clearly envisioned a program of extending the message of his sacrifice and the invitation to submit to his reign. Knowing of his own departure, he gave his disciples the stimulus to hope for his return and reason to pursue his purposes until he did.

By these two sacraments, then, the Lord provided for the initiation and the nurture of the believer in the family of God. By baptism the believer declares his or her faith in Jesus Christ's gift of forgiveness of sin; and by the public expression of dependence upon the life of Christ the believer maintains unity with Christ and his people.

The Mission of the Church

The Bible indicates that the church that gathers must also be the church that scatters. The two callings—worship and mission—are inextricably united. They create a spiritual rhythm for the Christian life. There is no proclamation to the world without a distinct community to do the proclaiming. And at the same time, the call to come to Christ is an invitation to men and women to enter into this new community, distinct from the world. They can learn of Christ only with Christ's people, the church.

In recent years, people inside as well as outside the church have come to think of the church as an instrument of human progress or of social revolution. Somewhere people got the notion that the church is supposed to be a means of achieving something worthwhile in the secular world, something that secularism can measure and approve. In other words, the church is a means to a higher end.

Few people, however, think of the church as an indispensable means to life's highest reality. It is something like catching a plane for Chicago. That is one way to go. But you might drive or catch a train. You could even walk. The plane will get you there, but it is not absolutely essential.

Christians, however, believe that the church is more like an orchestra for a symphony. The symphony can exist in the composer's mind and on paper, but it remains an abstraction until the one thing necessary to make it real for hearers—namely, an orchestra—is found. The composer may have a lawn mower or a dishwasher. Both are excellent instruments for other purposes, but neither was designed to perform a symphony. Only an orchestra will meet that need.

In the same way, only the church serves to carry the good news of salvation through Jesus Christ. Men and women may join the church or remain outside, but they are not at liberty to change the church into something it was not designed to be. Like an orchestra, it fulfills its purpose only by being what it is.

And what is the church in the world? It is the body of Christ. It is God's answer to human need. It is light in the midst of darkness.

The Bible often links the mission of the church to the mission of God. The God of the Bible, like a shepherd, goes forth in search of lost and wounded sheep. He called Abraham to leave his kindred and promised not only to bless him but also to bless other nations through him (Gen 12:1-3). He sent Moses to his oppressed people in Egypt and delivered them from slavery. He sent a succession of prophets with promises and warnings for his people. Then at last, "in the fullness of time," he sent forth his Son.

The mission of the Son was the mission of all missions. During his public ministry, Jesus said he had come to seek and to save the lost. He sent forth his disciples to preach, teach and heal. Then, after his enemies succeeded in nailing him to a cross, he sent his Spirit to empower his disciples to fulfill his final command: "Go into all the world and preach the good news" (Mk 16:15). Jesus' mission was a model for his disciples. "As the Father sent me," he said, "I am sending you" (Jn 20:21). The mission of the church arises from the mission of Jesus.

There is, however, a significant difference. By his death and resurrection Jesus Christ secured the salvation of men and women; by the power of his life-giving Spirit the church announces the salvation that Jesus secured.

We call this witness of the church *evangelism.* The term is often misunderstood. It comes from a Greek word that means to announce the *euangelion,* the good news. In Christianity that can only mean the good news about Jesus' death and resurrection and gift of the Spirit.

This is how worship and witness are linked: in worship we praise God for his salvation; in evangelism we tell others about this same salvation.

The Quaker scholar Elton Trueblood once compared evangelism to fire. Evangelism occurs, he said, when Christians are so ignited by their contact with Christ that they in turn set other fires. It is easy to determine when something is aflame: it ignites other material. Any fire that does not spread will eventually go out. A church without evangelism is a contradiction in terms, just as a fire that does not burn is a contradiction.[2]

In the end, then, Billy Sunday's down-to-earth wisdom is only a half-truth. The church as a religious institution cannot guarantee the life of God to a worshiper. But as the community of faith that God intended, the church can make available the Word of God and the grace of God for followers of Christ everywhere.

16
FORGIVEN SINNERS

Ew York City has the Statue of Liberty, symbol of the ideal of the French Revolution: freedom from the oppression of unjust regimes, both civil and ecclesiastical. Rio de Janeiro has the statue of Christ the Redeemer, symbol of the message of Christianity: deliverance from enslavement to sin, death and fear.

The Statue of Liberty rises in massive splendor out of New York Harbor and extends her light of freedom to all who come to American shores. Christ the Redeemer stands atop 2,300-foot Mount Corcovado. He is depicted not on the cross, as one might expect in a largely Roman Catholic country, but with outstretched arms, inviting the whole bustling city below to look to Jesus Christ for salvation.

When Christians say, "Look to Christ," what do they mean? What is salvation? And how do we receive it?

The Meaning of Salvation
Salvation is one of the basic ideas of Scripture, from the sacrifices of Abraham in Genesis to the songs of the redeemed in Revelation. In the Old Testament, salvation is closely linked with redemption. It

means deliverance from some sort of confinement, such as slavery. In Israel's history, this release is nearly always from some physical or political tight spot.

The best example is the deliverance from the bondage in Egypt, the exodus. After Moses stretched out his hand over the threatening waters and led the children of Israel "through the sea on dry ground," they saw the Egyptian forces—chariots and horses—swept into the sea. And they knew they were free. "That day the LORD saved Israel from the hands of the Egyptians" (Ex 14:29-30). Once delivered, Moses and the Israelites sang: "The LORD is my strength and my song; he has become my salvation" (Ex 15:2).

This miraculous deliverance became the foundation of Israel's hope through scores of other dangers during the age of the judges, the kingdom of David and Solomon, and the titanic struggles with Assyria and Babylon. These experiences taught Israel to sing:

No king is saved by the size of his army;
   no warrior escapes by his great strength.
A horse is a vain hope for deliverance;
   despite all its great strength it cannot save.
But the eyes of the LORD are on those who fear him,
   on those whose hope is in his unfailing love. (Ps 33:16-18)

Israel came to see that liberation is never the work of human beings; God alone saves.

The New Testament, like the Old, does not define salvation. It chooses instead to proclaim it as an accomplished fact. In the New Testament, however, salvation is no longer a physical and provisional deliverance, such as an escape from some military threat. It is total liberation, ultimate deliverance (Rom 1:16).

This deliverance, granted by God, is never described in terms of some gradual ascent to a higher level of existence. It is always pictured as a sharp break with the past, such as life from the grave. A saved person moves dramatically from enslavement to liberty, from death to life. That is salvation.

But what are people saved from? They are saved from sins (Mt

1:21), from condemnation (Jn 3:17), from death (Lk 6:9) and from the wrath of God (Rom 5:9). Throughout its pages the New Testament stresses that no threat is as serious for a person as the disapproval of God. Understandably, then, salvation consists fundamentally of the recovery of peace with God. It is the deliverance from the condemnation of God and entrance into the favor of God.

When we think of the gift of salvation in personal terms, we can distinguish three fundamental aspects: initial salvation, continued salvation and completed salvation. Initial salvation embraces all that God does in a believer's life to initiate the life of God in the soul and establish a special, new relation with God. Continued salvation is a way of describing the believer's spiritual life, how a person grows and matures in his or her relation with God. Completed salvation deals with the finished product, what God intends for a believer in his or her perfected state.

In this chapter we want to concentrate on initial salvation, how the deliverance from fear and impotence and sin and death begins. In the next chapter we will examine how it continues and, in chapter twenty, how it is completed.

Estranged from God, men and women face two basic spiritual needs. First, they need to be restored to God's fellowship. They are guilty before God, and somehow they must find forgiveness. Second, they need power to change. Their sin reveals their spiritual impotence. If life is to be different, someone will have to show them how to overcome their failures and find the strength to be new persons. In short, men and women need something done *for* them and something done *in* them.

Justification by Faith

One way to describe initial salvation is by a term often used by the apostle Paul: *justification*. Paul asks whether a person can be justified before God by strictly observing the Jewish law. Or, to put it another way, can sinners be considered saints in God's eyes if they determine to obey God's commands?

The term *justify* comes from the courtroom; it refers to a legal verdict. It means "acquit." It is not concerned with a person's righteous character, but with a person's relationship to God and his just law. Are people who have sinned in the past acquitted by God if they have kept the law's commands? Paul answers no. No one can keep the law in every point. That is impossible.

How, then, can a person be justified? Is there some other way than keeping the commands of God? Yes, says the apostle. In the Jewish law itself there is a provision for the offender to offer sacrifice to God for sin. In this way sin can be canceled and the spiritual rebel forgiven. Drawing, then, upon the language of the sacrificial system, Paul asserts that the death of Jesus was a sacrifice for sin. He describes it as an "expiation" or a "propitiation" (Rom 3:25).

For generations Christian scholars have debated the meaning of these two terms. *Expiate* is a verb that has as its object not a person but a thing. The purpose of sacrifice, then, is to expiate sin. The offering of a sacrificial victim wipes out sin; it cancels sin so that it no longer stands between the offender and God.

Propitiate, however, has as its object a person. It means to appease an offended person so that he or she is willing to forgive. In pagan religious language, the word referred to ways to placate the gods, who often broke out in fury against human beings. Such imagery compelled some scholars to reject the term for Christian theology, lest the sacrifice of Christ suggest that God is some capricious pagan deity. These scholars preferred *expiate.*

The term *expiate,* however, has significant weaknesses. It makes sin a thing that can be removed or erased. The heart of sin, as the Bible presents it, is the broken relationship between people and God. This alienation must be overcome. It requires some act that restores fellowship between God and rebels. It is not a question of the removal of some "thing," but a question of enmity and guilt.

Propitiate has the advantage of highlighting the personal effects of sin and the necessity of turning aside the wrath of God. The beauty of the gospel, according to Paul, is precisely in this fact: God himself offered Jesus as a propitiation for spiritual rebels. Justice and mercy met at Jesus' cross.

Through the course of Christian history, no one has seen this doctrine of justification more clearly than Martin Luther. The son of a Saxon miner, Luther had hopes of becoming a lawyer, until one day in 1505 he was caught in a severe thunderstorm. A bolt of lightning slapped him to the ground. Terrified, Luther called out to Catholicism's patroness of miners, "St. Anne, save me! And I'll become a monk."

Luther kept that vow. Obsessed with guilt, he entered the Augustinian monastery at Erfurt and proved to be a zealous monk. He pushed his body mercilessly, sometimes fasting for three days, sometimes sleeping without a blanket in freezing weather. Nothing seemed to relieve his tormented soul. No amount of penance, no soothing advice from his superiors could still Luther's conviction that he was a miserable, doomed sinner.

Relief eventually came through the Scriptures. Assigned to the chair of biblical studies at the University of Wittenberg, Luther became fascinated with the words of Christ from the cross, "My God, my God, why have you forsaken me?" (Mt 27:46). Christ forsaken! How could our Lord be forsaken? Luther felt himself forsaken, but he was a sinner. Christ was not. The answer had to lie in Christ's identification with sinful humanity. Was he forsaken in order to bear the punishment required by human sin?

Such questions opened before Luther a bold new picture of God. Finally, in 1515, while pondering the apostle Paul's letter to the Romans, Luther came upon the words: "For therein is the righteousness of God revealed from faith to faith: as it is written, The just shall live by faith" (Rom 1:17 KJV).

Here, at last, was Luther's answer to spiritual uncertainty. "Night and day I pondered," Luther later recalled, "until I saw the connection between the justice of God and the statement that 'the just shall live by faith.' Then I grasped that the justice of God is that righteousness by which through grace and sheer mercy God justifies us through faith. Thereupon I felt myself to be reborn and to have gone through open doors into paradise."

New Life in Christ

Luther's reference to a rebirth is appropriate. Another way of viewing initial salvation is captured in the term *regeneration*. It means new life or a new birth. The apostle pointed to this reality when he wrote: "God, who is rich in mercy, made us alive with Christ even when we were dead in transgressions" (Eph 2:4-5). When Christians are saved, they are "born again" into a new spiritual realm of existence.

When a person is regenerated, she is fundamentally changed. She is made alive to the life of God. What she once found repugnant becomes a source of pleasure. She discovers a new sense of values, a new lifestyle, a new understanding of herself, a new creative energy. These are all evidences of God's Spirit within. A true believer is simply a new person.

This new outlook echoes in one of our familiar hymns:

> May the mind of Christ my Savior
> Live in me from day to day,
> By His love and power controlling
> All I do and say.

> May the Word of God dwell richly
> In my heart from hour to hour,
> So that all may see I triumph
> Only through His power.[1]

This rebirth is no gradual process. It is a spontaneous, creative act of God. There is usually some preparation for it and some development of it, but the birth itself is spontaneous. A person is either alive to God or she is not. He is either a Christian or he is not.

"It may be hard," C. S. Lewis once said, "for an egg to turn into a bird; it would be a jolly sight harder for it to learn to fly while remaining an egg. We are like eggs at present. And you cannot go on indefinitely being an ordinary decent egg. We must be hatched or go bad."[2]

There is, of course, a difference between regeneration itself and the awareness of it. The first is an act of God in the soul. The second is a conscious personal response. Not everyone is immediately aware of the act of God. That is the reason one Christian should never insist that her experience be the standard for all others within the Christian community. Not everyone is immediately conscious of the influence of the Spirit in regeneration. The issue is not the way a person is regenerated but the fact of a person's regeneration.

Shortly before he was assassinated, Martin Luther King Jr., speaking in Los Angeles, chose to close an address by quoting an old slave preacher who said,

> We ain't what we ought to be,
>
> and we ain't what we want to be,
>
> and we ain't what we're going to be
>
> but, thank God, we ain't what we was.

That is true, too, of the genuine Christian.

This initial salvation, which restores a believer to God's fellowship, can be considered from God's side and from the human side. There is an attitude that God reveals, and there is a response required of men and women.

Amazing Grace

God's attitude and work in human salvation is captured in the word *grace.* While it is clear throughout the Bible that men and women must accept God's offer of salvation, this decision is never a basis of boasting. Human achievement and pride are forever eliminated from salvation by God's grace, his surprising love for the unlovely.

The story of the saving work of God, which binds the various books of the Bible into a unified whole, is an account of the grace of God. Without grace there would never have been a chosen people, no story of salvation to tell.

The Old Testament term for grace, *chesed,* often translated "steadfast love," stands for God's continuing faithfulness to his covenant people. The psalmist taught Israel to sing:

> O give thanks to the LORD, for he is good,

for his steadfast love endures for ever.
O give thanks to the God of gods,
for his steadfast love endures for ever.
O give thanks to the Lord of lords,
for his steadfast love endures for ever. (Ps 136:1-3 RSV)

It was God's grace that called Israel out of Egypt, and it was grace that would not let Israel go (Ex 15:13). The grace of God, then, is not a thing. It is God's attitude toward men and women. It is a personal relationship that God establishes and maintains.

The New Testament term *(charis)* underscores God's redemptive love, which is always active in rescuing rebels and restoring them to his wealth and favor. The apostle Paul, as perhaps no other person, probed the depths and wonder of God's love. He saw Israel's rejection of Jesus Christ as the climax of a long history of unbelief and apostasy. But "the stone the builders rejected has become the capstone" (Ps 118:22). Jesus Christ, once rejected and crucified, is the basis of a new covenant open to all people. Anyone can now be justified freely "by [God's] grace through the redemption that came by Christ Jesus" (Rom 3:21-24). Forgiving love, then, is the fountain of every other gift of grace flowing from the favor of God.

The human response to this initial salvation—including justification and regeneration—is captured in the term *conversion.* The word appears in many contexts today; Christians have no monopoly on it. People can be converted from democratic convictions to communism, or from conservative economic views to liberal ones.

In the Christian faith the term takes special significance only in the new direction of a person's change. A believer shifts from loyalties that are essentially selfish to loyalties that are directed toward Christ. A Christian is converted from a self-driven life to a Christ-controlled life. That is the important point.

Repentance and Faith

In Christianity, conversion always has two basic elements; one is negative, the other is positive. The negative note appears in the term *repentance;* the positive note sounds in faith.

The Christian concept of repentance springs from two biblical terms. In the Old Testament, the Hebrew word suggests some sort of "turning." In the New Testament, the Greek word indicates some "change of mind." So the Christian idea of repentance carries both ideas. It is a turning from the old way of life, dominated by selfish and sinful passions. And it is a change of mind—a new attitude—about God and Christ, and the direction of one's own life.

Repentance should never be confused with penance. That was an unfortunate error committed by Christians throughout the Middle Ages. They took Jesus' call to repentance in preparation for the kingdom (Mt 4:17) as an obligation to perform acts of self-denial in order to gain grace and find forgiveness. True repentance, however, is more inward than it is outward. It begins with the repudiation of one's own spiritual worth and only then moves to any expression of self-denial.

Genuine repentance is also always linked with faith. They are flip sides of the same coin. As repentance is an inward turning from the old life, so faith is the inward direction of the soul toward God, the Source of the new life. This faith is more than assent to the truths of the gospel. As we have seen, personal Christian faith moves beyond assent to personal trust in Jesus Christ as Savior. It is the essence of the relationship between the believer and God.

John Paton, pioneer missionary to the New Hebrides Islands, was once translating the New Testament into the language of the islanders. He could find no word, however, to translate *faith.* One day, after long hours of work, he slumped in his chair, exhausted. "I'm so tired," said Paton; "I feel like resting all my weight on this chair." Instantly, he sat straight up and yelled, "Praise God, I've got my word!" That is it. Faith means *putting all your weight* upon God. It is complete trust and commitment.[3]

Christians contend that "looking to Christ" in that sense brings salvation, a liberty that the Lady in New York Harbor has never known.

17
THE FAMILY LIKENESS
THE CHRISTIAN LIFE

Once, as I rode out into the woods for my health, in 1737," Jonathan Edwards writes in his *Personal Narrative,* "having alighted from my horse in a retired place, to walk for divine contemplation and prayer, I had a view of the glory of the Son of God. The person of Christ appeared ineffably excellent. I felt an ardency of soul to be emptied and annihilated; to lie in the dust, and to be full of Christ alone; to trust in him; to live upon him; to serve and follow him."[1]

Unfortunately, about all that many Americans recall about Jonathan Edwards is his sermon "Sinners in the Hands of an Angry God." That has erroneously established his reputation as a hellfire-and-brimstone Puritan revivalist. That is tragic, because the man was not only one of America's great minds but also—as this quotation reveals—a great soul.

Edwards reminds us that the Christian life is more than doctrines to confess; it is also a Person to follow. But how does faith tap this knowledge of God? What does the Christian life look like?

Sinners and Saints

As we have seen, people ordinarily suffer from two fundamental afflictions. They are estranged from God, and they are spiritually sick. They need to be reconciled to God, and they need to be made whole.

The salvation of God, as we experience it initially, is God's remedy for humanity's estrangement from God. It provides a way of reconciliation through the death and resurrection of Jesus Christ. Human beings may be justified in God's sight and receive the new life of the Spirit, but they must surrender all attempts at self-justification and trust in God's forgiveness. That is the beginning of salvation's story.

The Bible indicates that the transforming work of God only begins when a person experiences the birth of faith. As with any infant, the new life must then be protected and nurtured and exercised. That is what the Christian life is all about.

In one sense Christian believers are saved instantaneously—delivered from the deadly consequences of life without God. But in another sense they are not yet saved. They are not yet the persons God had in mind when he intercepted them in their mad scramble toward ruin. They are not completely freed from the sin that persists in their thoughts and values and actions. So we say, "Believers are being saved."

That is why the apostle Paul speaks at times of people "who are being saved," just as he does of "those who are perishing." Believers have not yet reached heaven any more than unbelievers have reached hell (1 Cor 1:18). The word for this process of salvation is *sanctification*.

Unfortunately, the term creates problems because it sounds so religious. It is related to the term *holiness* because in the Bible "to sanctify" means "to make holy." So a saint is a "holy one." But who wants to be a saint? "Holy" people intimidate us. When we hear *holy* we usually think of "holier-than-thou," and we often confuse *sanctified* with *sanctimonious*. As a result, we tend to associate the biblical expressions with some artificial and sometimes hypocritical religious person. And none of us wants to be that!

If we want to understand the Christian life, we will have to work our way through this problem. The best place to begin is with some old ideas. In the Bible the basic meaning of the word *holy* is "separate" or "different." In Old Testament times something "holy" was set apart or reserved for God's use. Sacrificial animals, for example, were holy. In the same way certain days were *sanctified,* which means they were set apart for the worship of God.

So when the New Testament calls Christians "saints," it simply means that they are intended for God's special use. Whether singing his praise in the sanctuary or resisting injustices in the world, Christians are "the people of God."

It might help to think of the way Jesus was different. He did not put on pious airs. When he came into town, the common people welcomed him. They found him attractive and winsome. How was he different? Certainly not in his religiosity. He had character, integrity and purpose. He was not enslaved to peer pressure or public opinion. As he helped people in agonizing need, he was remarkably free of self-interest. When tempted to think of Number One, he resisted the temptation and submitted to something higher in life. He had come, he said, to do the Father's will.

A close look at Christ is important because the first way the New Testament describes holiness is in terms of "Christlikeness." Paul tells the Corinthians, "We . . . are being transformed into his likeness with ever-increasing glory, which comes from the Lord, who is the Spirit" (2 Cor 3:18). Peter stresses the same idea in his first letter. He urges his readers: "Just as he who called you is holy, so be holy in all you do; for it is written: 'Be holy, because I am holy' " (1 Pet 1:15-16). Sanctification, then, is day-by-day growth in Christlikeness.

The Law of Holiness

Life itself seems to reveal a law of likeness. A person becomes what he or she admires. In nature, for example, the sunflower turns its face to the rising sun and grows by weaving the sunbeams into the fabric of its existence. The parallel in Christian experience is holiness. When men and women make Jesus Christ the center of their loyalty and love, they grow in Christlikeness.

American literature holds a memorable illustration of this law. It comes from Nathaniel Hawthorne's story "The Great Stone Face." A boy named Ernest grew up in a beautiful valley hidden among the mountains. On a high mountain crag overlooking the valley, the rocks took the form of a human face, a strong, noble face that inspired wonder in anyone who looked at it intently.

In the valley was a legend that someday a great and noble person who would resemble the face on the mountain would return to the valley. He would be a native son who had grown up there, had gone out and achieved fame in the world outside, and then had returned to bring wonderful benefits to people in the valley.

Ernest's mother explained this legend to her little son, and he grew up looking often toward the mountain face and longing for the great one to come. By and by, when he was a young man, the news spread that the legend was about to be fulfilled. A son of the valley had gone out and made a fortune and was now returning to spend his last years with his old neighbors. Rumors swept through the valley that he looked exactly like the face on the mountain. In due time he arrived and the crowd cheered, believing the prophecy had come true. When Ernest saw him, however, he was disappointed. The calculating profile had none of the nobility that characterized the Great Stone Face.

Time passed and Ernest grew older. His neighbors sought him out for counsel and comfort. Inspired by the face on the mountain, he proved to be a friend of all. Every few years a new rumor arose; another aspirant would come back to the valley, the supposed fulfillment of the legend. The second to arrive was a famous general from the wars, "Old Blood-and-Thunder." The third was a statesman aspiring to his country's highest office, "Old Stony Phiz." Each time, filled with wishful thinking, the excited crowd was sure that the long-awaited benefactor had arrived; but each time, as Ernest looked to verify the report, he was disappointed.

Finally, there returned to the valley a poet whose exalted verse

Ernest had come to admire. Maybe he was the fulfillment of the great hope. But when Ernest suggested the idea, the poet quickly denied it. He explained that while his words reflected the noble image, his life had not always done so. One evening, however, as the poet sat with the other neighbors and listened to Ernest offer encouragement and help to his friends, the sunset glow upon the prophetic face on the mountain shone also on Ernest's face, and the poet cried out, "Look! Look! Ernest is the likeness of the Great Stone Face!" Then all the people looked and saw that what the deep-sighted poet had said was true.

That is one way of describing the Christian life. It is growing in Christlikeness.

A second way of looking at sanctification, the Christian's progress in faith, is through a new realm of existence. The believer, we read, is "in Christ." What does that mean? We might compare the image to weightlessness. When the space programs of the United States and the Soviet Union were launched, space travelers encountered an unusual reality, life in weightlessness. It was a whole new realm of existence and called for special equipment to guarantee human survival in a world without gravity. Scenes of life in the realm of weightlessness soon became common to television viewers, with pictures of food or tools or even human beings drifting aimlessly about a spaceship.

Life in Christ

The new realm in which believers find themselves is "in Christ." The apostle Paul uses the expression in his letters no fewer than 160 times. It is obviously fundamental to his view of the Christian life. "If anyone is in Christ," he writes, "he is a new creation; the old has gone, the new has come!" (2 Cor 5:17). The believer's spiritual life begins "in Christ" and continues "in him." Paul urges the Colossians: "Just as you received Christ Jesus as Lord, continue to live in him, rooted and built up in him" (Col 2:6-7).

What the apostle intended by this expression is not entirely clear. Adolf Deissmann was the German scholar who first drew attention to the importance of the phrase in the theology of Paul. He held that the expression indicates a spiritual atmosphere in which the believer lives—something like a bird's life in the air, or as we have suggested, astronauts in weightlessness.[2]

Other scholars questioned an interpretation that makes Christ an atmosphere rather than a person. They prefer to think of Christ's authority or his power to command obedience. To be in Christ is to be in submission to his will.

The truth of the matter probably lies in the combination of the two views. A Christian is in Christ in the sense that she is united to him by faith and is brought increasingly into the sphere of his sovereign authority. In this new spiritual environment the Christian finds spiritual life and maturity.

Free at Last

A third way to think of the Christian life is freedom from the slavery of self-centeredness. Once in conversation with some proud Jews, Jesus said, "If you hold to my teaching, you are really my disciples. Then you will know the truth, and the truth will set you free."

"We are Abraham's descendants," they replied, "and have never been slaves of anyone."

"I tell you the truth," said Jesus, "everyone who sins is a slave to sin. . . . if the Son sets you free, you will be free indeed" (Jn 8:31-36).

Anyone who has ever tried to stop smoking or lose weight or control personal passions in any way will know what Jesus meant. Our appetites, our ego, our greed—these are like thick-walled prisons to anyone who has tried to find deliverance.

This is not the contemporary view of personal freedom, I know. Most moderns think that freedom is life without responsibility or commitments, a rootless lifestyle free to follow the least whim or impulse. Surely that is the route of happiness. Some fledgling poet caught the mood in a bit of verse:

> I'm tickled to death I'm single.
> I'm tickled to death I'm free.

I've got my independence.

I've got the front door key.[3]

As long as we think of freedom in terms of freedom from restraints, we will never understand Jesus. This contemporary gospel had no part in his thinking. He held a more realistic view of human nature. He knew that the person who is completely free to do as he pleases is soon a slave to some personal passion.

Jesus points instead to the freedom to pursue a purpose. The importance of this freedom is apparent all around us. Driving through some small town, we may well find Main Street bisected by a set of railroad tracks. A bell rings and red lights flash as a bar drops across the highway. Within a few seconds a powerful passenger train roars by, thundering west on two narrow rails. What is freedom for that train?

Or change the scene. When our children were youngsters, we had a tropical fish aquarium. With a shaft of light above and air bubbles supplying oxygen, the fish could swim gracefully around the aquarium and give the children great enjoyment. Once in a while, however, we would come home and find a swordtail or an angelfish out on the floor near the aquarium—dead as a mounted moose. What was freedom for that fish?

Freedom, you see, is the condition that allows us to fulfill the purpose behind our creation. As long as we insist on making life a fulltime "ego trip," we will never know freedom. As the train was made for the rails, as fish were made for water, we were made for God. That is why Augustine, the early church pastor, once said, "Slavery to God is perfect freedom." And that is why Charles Wesley wrote: "My chains fell off, my heart was free; / I rose, went forth, and followed thee" ("And Can It Be That I Should Gain").

Trust and Obey

Is this transformation into Christ's likeness, this mounting strength "in Christ," this increasing freedom to follow Christ, the work of God, or is it the responsibility of believers?

We have often heard, "God helps those who help themselves." We have heard the axiom so often that we may think it comes from the Bible. It doesn't. It has an element of truth, no doubt, but it can also mislead us. We may be tempted to think of God as the great booster who helps us over the humps in life—something like the extra horsepower we need when life is all uphill.

But anyone familiar with the Bible will recognize that God is more than that, much more. He is not in the business of rubber-stamping our proposals and plans. He is the beginning as well as the end. He never surrenders the initiative to anyone. He is the first and the last. He is Lord.

Does that mean, then, that I am supposed to sit back and take it easy? Am I supposed to relax and wait for the skies to open? That doesn't sound like the apostolic letters. What about fighting the good fight, running the race and finishing the course?

The issue of "How much does God do and how much do I do?" is fundamental to the Christian life. This is not an abstract question. It touches almost every area of Christian experience. Take public worship. Am I obligated to be at the sanctuary every time the door is open? How will the church survive if I do not support its services?

Put this way, that sounds like an awesome burden for a Christian to carry. But would we want to flip the coin and argue the other side? God doesn't need our help. It really doesn't matter whether Christians support the church or not. God has hidden resources, and human failure will never frustrate his plans.

What is the solution to this problem? We find a possible answer in Colossians 1:24-29. Paul is speaking there about his preaching of the gospel. He sums up by saying, "To this end I labor, struggling with all his energy, which so powerfully works in me." He could have made the same point about prayer, or giving, or reading the Scriptures, or any other Christian activity, because the same truth applies. Paul preaches zealously because of the nature of the gospel, a mystery "now disclosed to the saints." It is nothing less than "Christ in you, the hope of glory."

The gospel announces that Christ has not only come to pay the awful price for sin on the cross. He has also come to live within his people. So believers are no longer confronted with commands from an outside master; they are children of God, imbued with the life of their Father. They have actually received his life and power. This is the gospel, and it is the resolution of the problem of our initiative or God's.

What specifically, then, does the Christian do to enlarge the life of God in the soul? Christians have always taken one of two positions on that question.

Some Christians tend to look to the ministry of the church for their growth in grace. We might call them institutional believers. They have been taught to believe that the grace of God is associated with the sacraments of the church. By faithfully attending church and receiving the teaching and counsel and sacraments of the institution that Jesus established, they hope to grow in their knowledge and likeness of him.

Other Christians take a more personal approach to growth in grace. They are less dependent upon the church and more inclined to practice personal spiritual disciplines. We might call these Christians individual believers. They tend to rely less on the church and more on the Bible for their knowledge of God and their concept of Christian conduct. They do not resist Christian gatherings, but they tend to see corporate Christianity as a means to the end of personal holiness.

The truth of the matter probably blends both of these emphases. The church strengthens our Christian faith by reminding us that God's purpose is a people who embody his truth and grace. The church lifts faith out of the inner world of the soul and plants it in a generation-spanning tradition sustained by the gospel. It insists that true faith arises from the great redemptive acts of God in history.

At the same time, the Bible reminds us time and time again that institutions without the renewing power of the Spirit within the soul are barriers to true faith. Many times in the past, faith in the gospel has had to resist Christian officials and traditions and ceremonies. Only an intensely personal relationship with God is capable of igniting the flames of spiritual renewal.

Christians of both commitments, however, have agreed that two practices are absolutely indispensable for Christian holiness. They are prayer and the reception of the Word of God.

Prayer is the conversation of the soul with God. It is the result of the new life brought by the regenerating Spirit. The apostle Paul expressed it this way: "You received the Spirit of sonship. And by him we cry '*Abba,* Father' " (Rom 8:15). Prayer, then, is a sign of the family likeness, the inward affinity of the soul for God.

Prayer takes many forms: praise, petition, intercession, thanksgiving, adoration. But whatever the expression, it is the means given by God to commune with him. So Christians pray corporately in public worship and personally in quiet communion.

The complement to prayer is the Word of God. Through the retelling of Scripture's story we discover what God is like and what he expects of us. And that for the Christian is food and drink. "Faith comes from hearing the message," wrote the apostle, "and the message is heard through the word of Christ" (Rom 10:17).

The one word for the Christian life is Christ. That is why Jonathan Edwards's lonely figure in a New England woods is a fit symbol for us all. Alone before God, he found that his deepest longing was to trust in Christ, to live in him, to serve and follow him.

18

THE DIFFERENCE FAITH MAKES
THE KINGDOM OF GOD

In Plato's *Republic* Socrates outlines his vision of the ideal commonwealth. When someone asks him where a person might find such a society, the wise man has to admit that no state on earth conforms to his ideal.

"But in heaven," he says, "perhaps there is a pattern of it laid up for the one who wants to behold, and beholding to found such a city in his own soul. It makes no difference whether it exists anywhere or ever will exist. For he would live in the ways of that city only and of no other."

Like Socrates, Christians believe that the kingdom of God is in heaven. The kingdom is simply the reign of God; it is the exercise of his right to rule. And that is supremely true in heaven.

But unlike Socrates, Christians proclaim that this sovereignty of God has appeared in human history. They got the idea from Jesus. He preached that his power over disease, and demons, and death itself demonstrated that authority from the Hidden World had appeared on earth. "The kingdom of God," he preached, "has come upon you" (Mt 12:28). He meant himself. He was more than an envoy of the Almighty; he *was* the Almighty—in disguise.

He often spoke of his presence as a light in darkness. "I am the light of the world," he said (Jn 8:12). And he taught his disciples how to share in his mission. "Let your light shine before men," he told them, "that they may see your good deeds and praise your Father in heaven" (Mt 5:16). They were ordinary people with the common failings of human nature, but under Jesus' influence they became reflectors of his light—envoys of his authority.

That is how the Christian mission began. Today believers look back over two thousand years, but they cannot escape that original mandate: "Let your light shine before men." What did Jesus mean? How are Christians light in the world? How is the kingdom of God infiltrating enemy territory?

The Shape of the World

Over the centuries and around the earth today, believers have lived and served Christ in a host of circumstances. Their mission is determined in part by the conditions they find in their world.

Both history and the contemporary scene reveal at least three fundamental conditions into which Christians are sent.

First, in some societies Christians are a small minority and their social influence is minimal. In these countries, as believers are faithful to the gospel, their way of life usually provides a sharp contrast with the world around them. They are subject to the same attitudes and reactions that minorities experience everywhere. But, in spite of their limited influence in the political and social arena, their church life is often dynamic and attractive to outsiders. It is often a model of social relationships, reflecting reconciliation and forgiveness under the lordship of Christ.

In general, this was the condition of the churches in the first three centuries of Christian history. They demonstrated for all subsequent generations of Christians that large numbers and positions of power in society are not essential for influence and impact upon the world.

Second, in other societies churches are a part of a long tradition of

Christian influence in public life, in government, politics and social customs. The acceptance of Christian behavior has become so widespread that a sharp contrast between the lifestyle of Christian churches and surrounding society has all but disappeared. Under these conditions it is not always clear to what degree Christians have "Christianized" society and to what degree society has "paganized" the church. In either case, Christians have access to public office and to other decision-making positions in the society.

These conditions prevail in subcultures of Christians here and there about the globe today; they were also the social context for the church throughout most of the Middle Ages. The Christian light was so successful in dispelling the darkness of paganism in much of the Roman Empire that men and women came to talk about "Christendom" and "Christian Empire" and "Christian nations" and "Christian culture." This success created Søren Kierkegaard's problem: How do you introduce Christianity to Christendom? Or if we shift the image, how do you let your light shine in twilight?

Third, in still other societies Christians live under the constant opposition of some anti-Christian force. This power is usually some ideology or some religion established by law or tradition. In these circumstances, such as in a Muslim state, the Christian mission is often reduced to a struggle for survival and Christians are treated as second-class citizens. Persecution, an ever-present threat, seriously restricts personal evangelism and public worship.

This third condition is common in the modern period of Christian history, when many political ideologies have arisen to challenge traditionally Christian societies. A sometimes subtle, sometimes blatant barrage of anti-Christian propaganda adds to the church's handicap. This criticism of Christianity is usually based on some real or supposed fault of the church in the past: its imperialism, anti-intellectualism, colonialism or otherworldliness.

Ideals of the Western World

In many Western countries this anti-Christian attitude comes not in the form of direct attack but in the quiet displacement of traditional Christian beliefs by secular values drawn from a pragmatic version of humanism. It is not difficult to spot the moral breakdown in the Western world. In the name of personal liberties the public media often ridicule marriage, while social agencies vainly try to find alternatives to disintegrating families. Most members of society think of life in terms of material wealth and comfort, but find their work almost devoid of meaning.

For millions employment is synonymous with boredom. And leisure hours are seldom filled with healthy recreation; they usually call for some vicious amusement associated with alcohol or drugs, chemical escapes from emptiness and anxiety. The old sense of community has all but disappeared. In most big cities millions live in utter loneliness. And over this whole scene the constant fear of some nuclear or environmental nightmare casts a hellish shadow.

What is the answer for this crisis? There is no shortage of proposed remedies. In the so-called free world nearly all of them reflect the secular values of the idea of Progress: politics, education and science. Nearly everyone assumes that Christianity has nothing to say.

Those who prescribe some political remedy or new legislative diet tend to forget that politics requires an accurate reading of the people governed. If a political system is unjust, exploitative and self-serving, it is usually a reflection of the people's own apathy or injustice. Enforcement of laws is limited by public morality. As long as people are greedy, dishonest, selfish and immoral, no political system can be entirely just. It can only treat the symptoms of social sickness.

Given this weakness in the political system, other people look to education to cure society's ills. In any democratic society education has a role to play. Fears feed on ignorance, and an informed citizenry is basic to the ballot. But education without faith, informed by a sense of justice, can develop only what is latent. It cannot change human nature. It can make a saint into an intelligent believer; or it can make a thief into a crafty burglar. It can teach the young to read the classics or to pore over pornography.

Practically the same criticism applies to science as a remedy for the moral crisis. Science has provided us with cures and comforts beyond the highest hopes of our ancestors. But as we have discovered, scientists can also refuse to assume responsibility for the results of their research, on the grounds that politics and morality do not fall within the realm of science. Science is supposed to be indifferent to moral considerations. It doesn't care whether a laboratory produces penicillin or plutonium, whether a computer stores literature or lies.

The nuclear age has raised troubling questions in the minds of common folk about the control of any science that endangers their lives, be it nuclear fission, genetic engineering, chemical contamination or any other.

Light in the Darkness

The Christian response to this moral crisis in the Western world is neither a program for a new society nor a withdrawal into an inner world of the spirit. Today, as always, Christians serve as light in the world. They insist that social problems are often moral problems, because human beings are bound by moral laws and societies must respect them.

If a community is to be healthy, it must recognize the sanctity of life, marriage and property. Leaders must administer justice impartially. People must consider promises binding. The state must be the servant of the people, not their master. It must make virtue easier than vice and punish crimes against its citizens.

This is no exhaustive list. It cannot be, because Christianity advocates no specific political program. Political needs vary from age to age; but Christianity is a way of life for all generations. It has grown through a host of political and social conditions. As G. B. Caird once said, as conscientious citizens, Christians are bound to take an interest in politics, but their Christian faith will not automatically tell them how to vote.

On rare occasions, a political issue may be so clear that all Christians ought to rally to one side of a dispute. But usually all available policies are imperfect by Christian standards, so equally loyal and sincere Christian citizens will arrive at conflicting convictions.

Christians are light in this darkness in two basic ways. First, they influence society at large by the light of the gospel. Second, they build the church, a special community in society.

Christians as light in the world face two basic responsibilities: they must keep the darkness from extinguishing the light, and they must extend their light into wider and wider realms of darkness.

Most Christians live in a world that repudiates their faith and behavior. We have come to call this resistance to the light "peer pressure." The pressure appears in small matters. In the neighborhood, on the job or in public schools the Christian rubs shoulders with people who drink too much, tell sexually suggestive stories, sanction racism and steal other people's property.

If Christians refuse to condone immorality or dishonesty, they often find themselves the target of ridicule. Immoral people always resent the example of moral people. A Christian's mere presence is a silent criticism of a questionable lifestyle, and a non-Christian never feels comfortable until the Christian offers some symbol of his or her approval of the immoral action. As a result, the non-Christian is always pressuring the Christian to accept sin. Evil is contagious. The Bible puts it bluntly: "Bad company corrupts good character" (1 Cor 15:33).

Social pressure can make life miserable for adults, but the greatest impact is on children and adolescents, who have less resistance to this kind of coercion. Many a teenager has sacrificed his or her future and health to avoid the rejection of peers. Christian parents who try to raise their youngsters by Christian values find that other children are often their most vicious opponents.

Fortunately, social pressure is never irresistible. The apostle Paul encouraged the Corinthian Christians with a reminder that temptation is common and God will not permit believers to be tempted beyond what they can bear. God himself provides a way to stand up under it (1 Cor 10:13). All great social advances have come from men and women who were unwilling to follow the herd.[1]

Respect for Life

Resistance to the darkness, however, is the least part of the Christian's life in the world. Christians have proved time and again that darkness can be turned to light. The world can be changed. Two examples from the past will demonstrate how Christian values can shape society.[2]

Take, first, the attitude toward life itself. In 1897 scholars unearthed the rubbish heaps of Oxyrhynchus in Egypt. Among the finds was a letter from an ordinary man of the first century. His name was Hilarion. He writes to his wife Alis: "If— good luck to you!—you do have a baby, and it is a boy, let it be. If it is a girl, put it out." By "put it out" Hilarion meant to get rid of it.

Now this is not a criminal talking. Hilarion seems to have been an ordinary decent citizen, even a loving husband. His attitude toward infanticide was common.

The same pagan attitude toward unwanted babies appears in Plato. In the *Republic* he sketches an ideal society. In this society, he says, marriage should be sacred. But what in the name of sanctity does Plato propose for marriage? He recommends that "the offspring of the inferior, or of the better when they chance to be deformed, will be put away in some mysterious unknown place, *as they should be.*"

Contrast Plato's attitude toward infants with Jesus' attitude. Jesus called little children to him, set them in the midst of his disciples and said, "The kingdom of God belongs to such as these" (Mk 10:14). The disciples did not miss his point.

In an early church manual called the *Didache* we can catch the Christian attitude: "Thou shalt not murder a child by abortion, nor kill one when it is born." Again in an anonymous letter to a Diognetus, written in the second century, the author describes the life of Christians: "Christians are not differentiated from other people by country, language or customs. . . . They marry and have children just like everyone else; but they do not kill unwanted babies."

Christians held that taking the life of an infant was sin. They knew that life is from God, and eventually the Roman world agreed with them. In A.D. 374, for the first time, it became a crime in the Roman

Empire to take the life of a child.

In modern times this ground had to be won anew by Christian missionaries who went to countries where the gospel had not yet penetrated society. Early in the nineteenth century, Baptist minister William Carey campaigned against the sacrifice of infants in the rivers of India. Later in the century, Scottish missionary Mary Slessor resisted the ritual murder of twins in Calabar. Examples from other countries abound.

If respect for an infant's life has come to be accepted in many cultures today, it is due at least in part to Christian influence. We have come to take many of these ideals for granted, but many of them owe their origin and spread to the Christian faith. The gospel brings a new tenderness to life.

The second example is Christianity's struggle against slavery. Many Americans are familiar with the Christian defense of slavery in the old South. But this conservative reaction to the challenge of abolitionism is only a small episode in the Christian story. It is a reminder that the struggle included, at times, opposition from within the Christian camp. But Christians' reflection of their own cultural setting in no way negates the argument that Christian light can penetrate the world's darkness.

The social system of the Roman Empire at the birth of Christianity depended upon slavery for nearly all of its labor, skilled and unskilled. Historian Edward Gibbon estimated that at the time of Emperor Claudius (A.D. 41-54) slaves made up half of the population in the Roman world.

The overthrow of that gigantic evil could not come overnight. Christians, in fact, like those in the old South, were part of the system. Not only did Christians live in a society supported by slaves, but large numbers of them were slaves themselves. Their critics claimed that Christians preached to the dregs of the population and that slaves were the means of Christianity's spread to other members of a household—carriers, as it were, of the disease.

The way the faith first modified the system is illustrated beautifully by Paul in his letter to a Christian master. He urges Philemon to receive back a runaway slave, now converted, "no longer as a slave, but better than a slave, as a dear brother" (Philem 1:16).

In a world half slave, half free, no one inside or outside the church envisioned an instantaneous overthrow of the system. In the church, however, believers took equality for granted. Inscriptions on early Christian tombs almost never indicate whether the body belonged to a free person or a slave. When the great persecution of the church swept across the empire, mistress and maid were confined to the same prisons and died in the same arenas.

The crumbling of the system in society did not begin until Constantine's conversion (A.D. 312) made official enactments against slavery possible. And other factors made them sensible. The first meager legislation against it is striking. It forbids the branding of runaway slaves on the face because "the face is formed in the divine likeness." Other ameliorating acts followed one by one. During these years the churches continued to insist that in Christ "there is neither Jew nor Greek, slave nor free" (Gal 3:28).

In one sermon on baptism from the fourth century we can readily capture the attitude. Gregory, pastor of the church at Nazianzus in Asia Minor (today's Turkey), told his people: "Do not, you rich, disdain to be baptised with the poor, nor you noble with the base, nor you masters with one till now your slave. . . . From the day that you are born anew, all the old marks disappear."

In the church "the old marks" may have vanished in a new birth, but in the Roman world they took a little longer. By the time of Emperor Justinian (A.D. 525)—after two hundred years of the "Christian" Empire—Christians at last succeeded in convincing Roman society that slavery was contrary to God's creative purposes.

Colonies of Heaven

This light upon the darkness of child abuse and slavery would have been impossible had there been no church to sustain it. The overthrow of evil came because individual Christians reinforced one another in the fellowship of the saints and because the Christian faith, nurtured in the community of believers, made the overthrow possible. The light of God's truth shines brightest in the church.

Jesus did not say to each disciple, "You, my friend, are the light." At times that may be true. The believer may have to stand for the truth alone. But he or she is always supported by the people of God who share the same unique quality, the power to illuminate darkness, made possible by contact with the Light. Jesus wanted to stress that corporate reality, so he said, "You [a plural pronoun] are the light of the world" (Mt 5:14).

It is true that the churches are often far from models of the kingdom of light. They are composed of struggling pilgrims on the way to the city. They have not yet arrived, but they have heard the good news of the kingdom: Jesus Christ is Lord! So the church serves as a colony in which believers can practice their faith, freed from unnecessary peer pressure and supported by a company committed to the same way of life and the same homeland.

This image of kingdom, colonies and pilgrims was familiar to early Christians. They could hardly escape it. When Augustus became the first emperor of Rome (27 B.C.), Roman armies had conquered a territory stretching from the North Sea to the Sahara Desert, and from the Atlantic Ocean to the Euphrates River. Within these borders peoples of many races and languages lived and worked in various states of culture, from the barbarism of central Europe to the educated elegance of Greece.

Such an empire had been won by force, but power alone was unable to unite it. Augustus saw that his only hope of maintaining imperial authority over this vast conglomeration lay in joining its diverse population by bonds of common interest and common loyalty. He had to spread Roman law, Roman culture, Roman ideas and the Roman way of life throughout the provinces.

In the past, Rome had settled communities of army veterans, called colonies, as garrisons in conquered territory. Augustus extended this practice by giving full Roman citizenship not only to settlements of veterans but also to important provincial cities and to men who had distinguished themselves in public service. These provincial communities held equal rights and privileges with the citizens of Rome itself. In return, they were expected to represent Rome and all things Roman to their neighbors, so that the Roman way of life might permeate their province. This policy proved extremely successful. In A.D. 212, Emperor Caracalla was able to issue a decree admitting all his subjects to Roman citizenship.[3]

During New Testament times, the city of Philippi, where Paul founded a church on his second missionary journey, was a Roman colony. When Paul later wrote to the church at Philippi and underscored the meaning of church membership, he had at hand an illustration his readers could easily understand. "Our citizenship," he wrote, "is in heaven." James Moffatt translates the statement even more strikingly: "We are a colony of heaven" (Phil 3:20).

We can easily extend the image: This world is an empire; its capital city is heaven; its emperor is Jesus Christ. But the Lord Jesus Christ has not yet subjected the world to his law, educated it in his ways or united it in loyalty to himself. To achieve all this, he has set throughout his empire colonies with all the rights and privileges of the kingdom of heaven and with his own authority and power at their disposal. Their responsibility is to represent the Lord and the Christian way of life to the world, until the light of the gospel permeates society and all peoples confess, "Jesus is Lord."

19
THE POINT OF PROVIDENCE
DESTINY

I t is sometimes difficult to resist the conclusion," said the indomitable British journalist Malcolm Muggeridge in 1974, "that Western Man has decided to abolish himself, creating his own boredom out of his own affluence, his own vulnerability out of his own strength, his own impotence out of his own erotomania."

Before four thousand participants at the International Congress on World Evangelization in Lausanne, Switzerland, Muggeridge traced his experiences in public life going back a half century to World War I. During those years, he said, he was told the war was to make the world "fit for heroes to live in." God was surely on Britain's side, and his spokesman, it turned out, was Woodrow Wilson. So in the columns of the *Manchester Guardian* Muggeridge thundered away about how the League of Nations would ensure peace if only everyone would disarm and institute democracy and education for all.

That seemed like the wise course to Muggeridge; he had been brought up to believe that the welfare state in accordance with the policies of Britain's Labor Party would bring Jesus' kingdom to earth.

When the Labor Party eventually gained ascendancy, to Muggeridge's surprise Jesus' kingdom failed to appear.

Disillusioned, Muggeridge turned his hopes for a better world toward the Soviet Union. "Managing to get myself posted to Moscow as a newspaper correspondent," said Muggeridge, "I soon realized that, far from giving a new vitality to liberty, equality, and fraternity, the Soviet regime was rapidly turning into one of the most absolutist tyrannies of history. Thenceforth I had no expectation whatsoever that man could perfect his own circumstances and shape his own destiny."[1]

Who would think of blaming Muggeridge for his pursuit of history's meaning? Here and there a philosopher tells us that "history has no meaning." But most people find that courageous skepticism unbearable. Like Muggeridge, they want to find some purpose in human existence. Where, they ask, is history going?

The Direction of History

Ever since the ancient Hebrew prophets found their people trapped between the threatening empires of Egypt and Assyria, people in what we have come to call Western civilization have held that life on planet earth does move with some purpose.

This is one of the major distinguishing marks of the Judeo-Christian faiths in the Western world: they believe that ultimate meaning courses through history. Or to make the point in religious terms, God works in and through human affairs to accomplish his own cosmic purpose. The major Eastern religions do not believe that. They teach, instead, that men and women must escape from history somehow in order to find life in the realm of the gods.

That is why some have called the liberal faith in human Progress and the Marxist ideology "Christian heresies." Both teach that life's meaning can be found in history, in the global triumph of democratic ideals or in the socialist state that follows the revolutionary overthrow of capitalism.

Winston Churchill, the redoubtable voice for democracy during

World War II, once traced the direction of progressive liberalism in the twentieth century. Addressing the Mid-century Convocation of the Massachusetts Institute of Technology, he noted that the human race entered this terrible twentieth century with confidence.

> We thought that with improving transportation nations would get to know each other better. We believed that as they got to know each other better they would like each other more and that national rivalries would fade in a growing international consciousness.

> We took it almost for granted that science would confer continual boons and blessings upon us. . . . In the name of ordered but unceasing progress, we saluted the Age of Democracy expressing itself ever more widely through parliaments freely and fairly elected on a broad, or universal franchise. . . . The whole prospect and outlook of mankind grew immeasurably large, and the multiplication of ideas also proceeded at an incredible rate.

Unfortunately, as Churchill confessed, this vision was not accompanied by any noticeable advance in the stature of the human being, "either in his mental faculties, or in his moral character. His brain got no better, but it buzzed the more."[2]

The whole liberal vision rested upon an optimistic view of human nature that brought personal freedoms to masses of people who had never before dreamed of contributing to their own destinies. But something happened to the dream. As Churchill said, the twentieth century saw man become "the sport and presently the victim of tides and currents, of whirlpools and tornadoes amid which he was far more helpless than he had been for a long time."

Among these tornadoes was the lightninglike spread of Marxism. Masses of people came to believe that Marxism's faith was more realistic than democratic liberalism. It looked not to humane politics but to economic laws. It believed in sin, in the enslavement of the dispossessed, in the exploitation of the poor. It traced the demon to property. The capitalists, owners of the means of making a living, were driven by greed to the exploitation of wage earners, the working classes. Conditions would go from bad to worse until the enslaved masses were driven to revolution, the violent overthrow of capitalism and the creation of a socialist regime.

Unfortunately, as Muggeridge discovered in the Soviet Union, in state after state liberators were quickly transformed into oppressors. Sin may have corrupted the old regime; but suddenly it appeared in a new one as well.

The history of the last two centuries will show how often Christians joined Muggeridge in singing the praises of Marxism. All people, including Christians, have a tendency to expect too much from earthly regimes.

The Christian faith has since its earliest days insisted, however, that the significance of history comes not from within the ebb and flow of time but from beyond history. God, who reveals himself to men and women in creation and the cross, holds the key to the mysteries of time.

The sovereign Lord of the universe takes a hand in ordinary history in two fundamental ways: he gives providential oversight to human affairs, and by direct intervention he will bring to an end the course of all human history. The first involves the doctrine of providence; the second embraces the doctrine of eschatology.

Divine Providence

As we have seen, the Living God of the Bible is transcendent. He is the Holy One who lives in unapproachable splendor. Yet he does not govern the universe by remote control. He takes a hand in world affairs and knows the passing thoughts of every man, woman and child.

The Bible teaches that God is involved in creation—not only in the original act of creation but also in the continuing work of creating. The Old Testament says that every movement of the stars, every change of the weather, every phase of the life cycle of the tiniest creature is directed by God, the Creator.

According to Psalm 104, the Lord

makes springs pour water into the ravines;

> it flows between the mountains.
> They give water to all the beasts of the field;
>   the wild donkeys quench their thirst.
> The birds of the air nest by the waters;
>   they sing among the branches.
> He waters the mountains from his upper chambers;
>   the earth is satisfied by the fruit of his work. (vv. 10-13)

This same God, who created and is sustaining all things, directs the affairs of individuals and nations. He is more than an idle spectator of the human drama; he directs rulers and prompts people. There is, as Cambridge historian Herbert Butterfield once said, "a kind of history-making that goes on over our heads." We call this history-making divine providence—God's guidance of human events according to his purpose and plan.[3]

The most dramatic depiction of this work of the Living God is in the message of the Hebrew prophets who spoke to the Assyrian and the Babylonian crises. As one empire after another sent its invaders surging across the barren wastes of the Middle East, these men of God traced the hand of God in the events.

First came Assyria, marching on northern Israel. And how did the prophet Isaiah interpret the invasion?

> Woe to the Assyrian, the rod of my anger,
>   in whose hand is the club of my wrath!
> I send him against a godless nation,
>   I dispatch him against a people who anger me,
> to seize loot and snatch plunder,
>   and to trample them down like mud in the streets. (Is 10:5-6)

Israel had sinned; so judgment had to fall. Assyria's invasion, then, was more than empire-building, more than one mighty kingdom's swallowing up a helpless smaller state. According to the prophets, this incursion into Israel's borders was a "club of God's wrath."

Early Christians read these prophecies and made them a part of their own Bible. From these Hebrew seers they learned to look at history morally. Like the Jews before them, Christians believe in a moral retribution at work in the very processes of time—a kind of judgment before the final judgment.

Judgment in History

This divine retribution appears primarily in the flaws that are built into human political and economic systems. People create institutions, and for a time they serve the purposes of their designers quite well. But something always goes wrong. All systems face time's withering test, and eventually judgment falls.

Time knows no favorites. People have tried a host of political structures: city-states, empires, republics, monarchies, parliaments, dictatorships, democracies, oligarchies. It doesn't seem to matter, for what falls under God's judgment in the course of time is not this or that system but human nature itself. Human nature seems to be marred by a fundamental flaw. Men and women cannot realize their own ideals. Time brings out the basic human willfulness, and the structure crumbles.

The French Revolution affords a vivid example of how quickly a liberal movement can degenerate into a totalitarian autocracy. Within ten short years after the storming of the Bastille, France stumbled through democracy, a republic, a reign of terror, an oligarchy and a dictatorship.

The Hebrew prophets taught—and Christians believe—that God's judgment in history falls heaviest on those who think of themselves as gods and fly in the face of providence by demanding that men and women worship their way of life. That was Assyria's sin. Assyria's rulers had no thoughts of serving God's purposes. Their heads were filled with visions of empire. They were convinced that their own right arm had gained the victory.

> As one reaches into a nest,
> so my hand reached for the wealth of the nations;
> as men gather abandoned eggs,
> so I gathered all the countries;
> not one flapped a wing,
> or opened its mouth to chirp. (Is 10:14)

But Assyrian arrogance was no frustration for God. Isaiah asks, "Does an ax raise itself against him who swings it?" (10:15). As soon as the Lord has used Assyria to bring Israel to its knees, he dealt with the haughtiness of the invaders.

Later in the prophetic era came Babylonia, sweeping down on Judah. Like Isaiah before him, the prophet Jeremiah called Nebuchadnezzar, the king of Babylon, God's *servant* (Jer 25:8-9). He had come to judge God's people, to bring them to their senses.

This is tough faith. It takes a special kind of person to see the hand of God in the suffering of one's own nation, especially at the hands of an empire that is no less ruthless or cruel. One prophet, Habakkuk, dared to raise that issue. His problem was that God seemed to wink at the wickedness of the invaders:

> Your eyes are too pure to look on evil;
>
>> you cannot tolerate wrong.
>
> Why then do you tolerate the treacherous?
>
>> Why are you silent while the wicked
>
>>> swallow up those more righteous than themselves? (Hab 1:13)

God never gives the prophet a full answer. He tells him that the Babylonians' day will come. Wickedness will not go unpunished. But the Lord has a purpose in the apparent tragedies of life. The man of God must rest assured that these sufferings are not the final answer. That will come in the end. Until then, the righteous person will live by faith in God, who is sovereign and just (Hab 2:2-5).

According to Isaiah, Jeremiah, Habakkuk and their colleagues, then, human history is a mighty drama that the Lord God is staging on the earth. The nations are as a drop in a bucket before God. He raises up one ruler and disposes of another. He is the judge of the nations.

Men and women, however, have trouble reading the signs of the times. God's wrath and mercy are mingled, so evidence of his judgment is always incomplete. He crushes wrong, but new wrongs appear. Only the future will reveal the full meaning of human experiences. God's sovereignty will be evident only in final judgment and renewal. History must find its meaning in its end.

History's Last Word

The term for this view of history is *eschatology*. It comes from the Greek word *eschaton,* meaning "last" or "the end." So the eschatological view of history stresses the conviction that God has the last word about history. In the words of the familiar spiritual: "He's got the whole world in his hands."

In the end God will manifest himself to all in a dramatically new way. The Christian holds that the meaning of history—human destiny, if you please—does not arise from within history itself. It must come from God, who participates in history but stands outside the human story.

Jesus introduced an unusual explanation of this sovereignty of God in his teaching about the kingdom of God. Jewish teaching of his time stressed a two-age view of history. The present age is under the authority of evil powers: sin and death and the devil. So men and women live in frustration and fear. But another age—the age to come—will someday break upon the people of God. Messiah will appear to free his people from the shackles of fear, oppression and death. Then they will know the peace and righteousness of God's kingdom.

Jesus apparently accepted this widespread Jewish view, but when he spoke of the kingdom, he gave it a strikingly new twist.

The expressions "the kingdom of heaven" and "the kingdom of the Lord" went back to the days of Israel's most illustrious monarch, King David, whose reign became a token of the Lord's rule. In the Psalms and Prophets God's covenant and promise to David point to the Lord's own faithful rule and the hope of the coming "advent" (or appearance) of the Lord's anointed servant— the Messiah.

Jesus drew upon this faith—not without some risks of misunderstanding—when he announced, "The kingdom of heaven is at hand." He made it clear that the kingdom *comes* to men and women; they do not create it. Men and women need not ask, "How can we establish the kingdom?" Their first concern should be, "How do I enter the kingdom? Am I ready for the kingdom?"

Jesus answered that question for his disciples by pressing the essential importance of faith in him. That was the surprisingly new note. Jesus indicated that his miracles and message were signs that the age to come had already appeared! The peace and righteousness of the kingdom were already available to anyone who trusted Jesus for liberation from moral failures, evil powers and fears of death.

At some future day this kingdom, this sovereignty of God, would be manifest for all to see, but for the moment any genuine believer, any person trusting in Jesus for deliverance, could find a foretaste. So according to Jesus, the kingdom is already present in human history, yet it will come someday in evident glory.

Martin Luther captured the idea for Christians when he paraphrased the Lord's Prayer, "Your kingdom come, your will be done":

> Grant that this Thy kingdom, now begun in us, may increase, and daily grow in power. . . . Help us that we may remain constant, and that thy future kingdom may finish and complete this Thy kingdom which is here begun.[4]

Christians have not always taken Jesus' message in this eschatological and intensely personal way. Some have tried to turn it into middle-class moral counsel, others into a plan for social revolution. But for most, Jesus' teaching, like his death and resurrection, is directed at the struggle of the soul in every age of history.

The most influential interpretation of human destiny in Christian history comes from an age of crumbling empires. At the dawn of the fifth century, people expected the Roman Empire to endure forever. They called it "eternal Rome." Suddenly, however, in the year 410, a barbarian warlord named Alaric besieged the city of Rome. All cries for mercy proved futile. Alaric and his Visigoth warriors charged through the gates and plundered the capital, palace by palace.

A short time later, when the hordes withdrew from the city, devastation and ruin were everywhere. Shocked refugees fled in all directions. Some of them arrived in North Africa, where they were welcomed by a slim figure with sharp features, Aurelius Augustine, bishop of Hippo.

As always in an event of such magnitude, people cried out for explanations. "Why? How could this happen? Were the gods angry? Is this a sign of the end of the world? What went wrong?" To answer such questions and give his people a reason to go on, Augustine set about to give an explanation for the rise and fall of empires—and the personal pleasures and tragedies of life. We call his book *The City of God.*

Augustine's interpretation reaches back into the distant past—to creation itself—and forward to the final hour of the human story. In this cosmic context he discovers two realities that unite and divide all history, two historical societies or cities that are now mingled by world events but are destined one day to be separated. Like Jesus' kingdom, then, Augustine's city is eschatological. History is determined by destiny.

What is the difference between the cities? It is a difference of faith and love. "Two cities," writes Augustine, "have been formed by two loves: the earthly by the love of self, even to the contempt of God; the heavenly by the love of God, even to the contempt of self. The former, in a word, glories in itself, the latter in the Lord. For the one seeks glory from men; but the greatest glory of the other is God, the witness of conscience."

Christians hold that all institutions of history—empires, religions, nations, families, tribes—are subordinated to the central issue of all history: How does a soul appear before God? Is it enslaved to personal passions and pride, or does it know the liberty of new loyalty to God? As Augustine put it in one sentence: "In this mortal life a man is trained for eternal life."[5]

Alternative Ways

The Christian view of history, which focuses upon the liberation of individual souls and the creation of a destined community, rejects two popular alternatives: the belief that the meaning of life comes in some escape from history and the belief that history provides the whole story of reality. Christians reject all escape routes *from* history as well as all utopias *in* history.

The view that men and women must find reality outside history is very common. According to Christopher Dawson, the influential Catholic historian, "This denial of the significance of history is the rule rather than the exception among philosophers and religious teachers throughout the ages from India to Greece and from China to Northern Europe."[6]

The escapist view is basic to most forms of Hinduism and Buddhism. If God is the constant Being, as compared to an incessantly shifting realm of human experience, then God, not history, must hold the meaning of existence. So to seek reality, human beings must carry the soul beyond time into the Great Other World.

The Christian faith shares with this escapist view the conviction that there is more to reality than we see. History itself does not contain all of history's meaning. Meaning, however, will not come from a journey of the soul beyond the particularities of human existence to some realm of universal truth. God's kingdom is not of this world, but it has nevertheless come to time and space. It is, in an important sense, part of our history. Jesus Christ was crucified *under Pontius Pilate*. The gospel is good news about events in time.

The second alternative to the Christian view, the belief that history holds the answer to life's mystery, is likewise common. It appears most often in some form of imperialism, either religious or political.

The ancient Roman Empire, for example, claimed to embody the meaning of human history. Major literary figures in ancient Rome speak repeatedly of the empire's "eternity" and "finality." Virgil, Polybius and Livy consider *Roma Aeterna* the culmination of a secular process.

Early Christians, however, were convinced that Rome was not eternal, and they consistently rejected Rome's pretensions to divinity. They did so because they knew that God alone, the Lord of all history, was worthy of worship.

And that is the same conclusion Malcolm Muggeridge reached. He, like millions of Christians before him, turned from the dreams of democratic societies and the nightmares of communist regimes and found life's meaning in Jesus Christ.

20
THE FINAL CURTAIN
THE END

fter World War II, Arthur Miller's play *Death of a Salesman* turned the spotlight on the emptiness of American values. Willy Loman, the salesman, was a backslapping, life-of-the-party type. He drifted through life convinced that to know the right people and to be well liked was the formula for success. He lived by this creed; he taught it to his sons. He carried the deception almost to the end. Before he died, however, his business associates, his boys and even Willy himself saw through the charade. He died an empty, broken man.

A journalist once asked Arthur Miller how he explained the power of the play. He said the story dealt with a problem we all face, "the fear that one has lied to one's self. . . . What the play does is to make the individual ask himself whether his rationalizations about himself are not leading him to an ultimate rendezvous with a dreadful reckoning."[1]

Eschatology
In the Christian vocabulary the word for this rendezvous is *eschatology*. It is the doctrine that God determines human destiny. Whatever

other powers we may meet in this life, God's power is final. He has the last word. Simple reflection will show that men and women encounter "the end" in two ways: in personal death and in history's final curtain. There is a personal end and a cosmic end.

Willy Loman is not alone. In our day men and women try in countless ways to camouflage death. We try to pretend that it is not a reality. We disguise it with our clever euphemisms. To avoid the term *death* we substitute "passed away," and for *cemetery* we speak of "perpetual family plots." When a loved one dies, we pay cosmeticians handsomely to make our relatives look "natural" just before we lay them to "rest." All of our games, however, fail to hide the harsh fact of death.

Humankind is mortal. That is rock-bottom reality. From the moment of birth, human beings are on the way to death. Perhaps the ancient prophet in Israel put it best: "All flesh is grass." It springs up, dries in the heat of the sun and is soon swept away and forgotten. Death is the only prediction we can make with absolute certainty about human history.

Men and women look at death in several ways. Science tells us that it is a natural thing. All living organisms die. Why should the human species escape organic disintegration? Humans simply share mortality with parakeets, rosebushes and beagles.

Most of us, however, know instinctively that death is more than a biological fact. It frightens us. The thought of death, our death, brings a sense of dread. We long to cling to life, and we consider death an intruder. It seems to rob us of everything worthwhile.

When the Bible calls death an "enemy," we know exactly what it means. It is an enemy, a vicious, dreaded enemy. What power, we ask, has written this irrational end into the human story? If death means that it is all over, why is the longing to go on echoing in my heart? Life on earth cries out for some sequel.

This yearning for life after death is all but universal. Not many people are willing to accept death in a matter-of-fact way. Sigmund Freud called the belief in life after death "the oldest, strongest and most persistent wish of mankind." You can find it in nearly all the world religions, ancient and modern.

Hindus look for absorption of the individual soul into the world soul. They think of it as a drop of water falling into the ocean. In most traditional religions of Africa, death is an unnatural event. The disembodied soul joins the spirit world, waiting to enter another body. In most religions life after death is shrouded in uncertainty, but the belief is still there.

Among the ancient Greeks, life after death was linked to "the immortality of the soul." They held—and many moderns share their view—that human beings are made up of two essential parts, a body that will be buried or burned at death and a soul that will survive the trauma called death. The soul is the indestructible component of human nature. It will live on in some shadowy existence after death.

In spite of what many people think, Christians have never shared this pagan view of immortality. The Christian view of the afterlife is shaped by Jesus Christ's attitude. In the four Gospels Jesus dominates death. He submits to it, but only on his terms. He was sent into the world, he says, to change the face of death.

Upon hearing of the death of one of his closest friends, a man named Lazarus, Jesus told his disciples that Lazarus was "asleep" and that he would go and wake him. When he arrived in Bethany, he told Lazarus's two grieving sisters, "I am the resurrection and the life. He who believes in me will live, even though he dies." Then, as though demonstrating his claim, he raised Lazarus from death (Jn 11:17-44).

Jesus claimed to control even his own death. He said he had power to lay down his life and power to take it again. He convinced his disciples, and he did just what he said. By rising from the grave, he revealed his power over death. That is what sent out his disciples preaching Christ as the way, the truth and the life of the Hidden World.

In Christianity, then, men and women are not by nature "immortal." God alone possesses "immortality." He alone dwells in "unapproachable light" (1 Tim 6:16). In the Christian faith human immortality is not innate; it is a gift from God available through Jesus Christ.

He "brought life and immortality to light through the gospel" (2 Tim 1:10).

The Return of Christ

Nowhere do Christians differ more sharply from their secular neighbors than in their special view of life and death. Apart from the Bible, modern men and women are inclined to think that a woman is alive so long as she moves about in some degree of health. When the woman's health begins to fail seriously, we say that she is dying.

The Christian, however, gives a sharply different meaning to the words *life* and *death*. A woman may be dead in the midst of life, or she may be alive in the midst of death. That is because death is linked to sin, and spiritual life is found in a restored relation to God. Death is existence in evil; life means communion with God.

For the Christian, physical death is a step into life. It is not a terminus, but a transition. It leads to a fuller experience of life with God.

In one of his books, the New Testament scholar A. M. Hunter relates the story of a dying man who asked his Christian doctor to tell him something about the place to which he was going. As the doctor fumbled for a reply, he heard a scratching at the door, and he had his answer. "Do you hear that?" he asked his patient. "It's my dog. I left him downstairs, but he has grown impatient, and has come up and hears my voice. He has no notion what is inside this door, but he knows that I am here. Isn't it the same with you? You don't know what lies beyond the Door, but you know that your Master is there."[2]

The approach of death often raises questions in people's minds. Sometimes Christians ask: What about those who die before the return of Christ? Do they go to be with Christ as soon as they die, or do they wait around in some disembodied condition until the resurrection, when Jesus returns to earth?

That sort of question assumes that conditions after death are essentially the same as on earth. As far as we are able to determine, however, life beyond death is beyond the earthly measurement of time. So any discussion of how much time elapses between death and resurrection is beside the point. All who die trusting in the Lord Jesus Christ die in his love and will probably be unconscious of any passage of time before Christ's return. The image of sleep that Jesus used of death is helpful here. Most of us are not conscious of the passing of time between our going to sleep and our waking in the morning.

In the one passage in the New Testament that offers an answer to believers troubled about their dead loved ones, Paul writes: "The dead in Christ will rise first. After that, we who are still alive and are left will be caught up together with them in the clouds to meet the Lord in the air. And so we will be with the Lord forever" (1 Thess 4:16-17). What Paul stresses here is not the condition of souls between death and resurrection but the result of resurrection—believers will be with the Lord forever.

In another letter Paul applies this truth to himself. "I desire," he says, "to depart and be with Christ" (Phil 1:23). That sounds as if Paul expected to be with Christ immediately after death. But later he writes: "We eagerly await a Savior from [heaven], the Lord Jesus Christ, who . . . will transform our lowly bodies so that they will be like his glorious body" (Phil 3:20-21). That suggests that believers will not be raised up for the new life of God's kingdom until Christ returns.

On the surface the two statements appear contradictory, but we must remember that earthly time is irrelevant beyond death. The Christian believer awaits the day when time itself will be taken up into God's eternity, when Christ will come to call to himself all who love him, both the living and the dead. So the timing doesn't matter. What does matter is Christ's triumph over death.

God's Ultimate Triumph

Not only does the Christian faith stress an individual's personal destiny, revealed in death and life after death; it also speaks directly to humankind's cosmic destiny.

The question has assumed unusual significance with the dawn of the twenty-first century. The spread of environmental pollution, the constant threat of nuclear radiation, the rapid depletion of the earth's resources—all these keep the question of humanity's ability to survive on planet earth at the center of public attention. Along with its stress on human stewardship of the earth, Christianity offers a constant reminder that history's finale is in God's hands.

Over the years Christian believers have tried to picture this ultimate disclosure of God's plan for the ages. In recent generations some have tried to draw up a calendar of the end-time events, much as one would plot the course of a war after the fact. But most Christians have acknowledged several major features of the end without attempting to treat biblical prophecy as one would human history.

The Apostles' Creed, confessed by Christians over the centuries and throughout the world, is content to speak of four aspects of the end of the age: (1) Jesus Christ shall come to earth again, (2) he shall judge the living and the dead, (3) human beings will be raised to life and (4) Christian believers shall receive "life everlasting."

These four aspects of the end are related to each other because they all relate to Christ and the gospel. Through his death and resurrection Jesus anticipated the final unraveling of history's mystery. But only at his return to earth will his work as the mediator of salvation be complete. It seems best to let these four major convictions guide our thinking along with Christians in other ages.

Where did Christians get the notion that Jesus Christ will return to earth some day? The answer can come from only one source: Jesus himself taught his disciples to look for his return. Mark 13 and its parallel passage, Matthew 24, are filled with traditional Jewish images and are therefore difficult to interpret in every detail, yet the basic point comes through clearly. Jesus expected to return to earth after his original departure, and he taught his disciples to look forward to that event. He linked it with the end of the world as we now know it.

In these passages Jesus underscored two themes. No one knows the exact time of this great event, but the primary responsibility of a disciple is to be ready for it. Each disciple must take the promise seriously and live in the light of it.

The New Testament writings themselves reveal how intently the early disciples looked for the coming of their Lord. They were a generation of believers on tiptoes. Their worship services were celebrations of his presence and promised appearing. Their preaching to the pagan world was fired by the hope of Christ's coming to right all wrongs and to overcome humankind's last enemy, death.

In the light of Jesus' teaching and the faith of the first disciples, the important question about the end is not "When?" or "How?" but "Who?" Who will be in control of human destiny? Who will be in charge when the secrets of human hearts shall be revealed? There can be only one answer to that question: Jesus Christ.

When Jesus Christ returns, he will complete his work of salvation by triumphing over the last enemy. He will give to all his people transformed bodies. Christian believers will be changed and made ready for the life to come.

Christians have always found a sure promise of this event in Jesus' own resurrection. The apostle Paul wrote that Christ had been raised from the dead as the guarantee that those who sleep in death will also be raised (1 Cor 15:20).

The apostle explained that the generation of Christians who are alive on the earth when this occurs will not die, but will simultaneously share in the transformation of their bodies. This glorification—as Christians call it—is necessary, because our present corruptible bodies of flesh and blood cannot inherit the incorruptible kingdom of God. So Paul declared: "Listen, I tell you a mystery: We will not all sleep, but we will all be changed—in a flash, in the twinkling of an eye, at the last trumpet. For the trumpet will sound, the dead will be raised imperishable, and we will be changed. For the perishable must clothe itself with the imperishable, and the mortal with immortality" (1 Cor 15:51-53).

This is the way John Donne pictured the event in his "Holy Sonnet VII":

> At the round earth's imagin'd corners, blow

Your trumpets, Angels, and arise, arise
From death, you numberless infinities
Of souls, and to your scatter'd bodies go,
All whom the flood did, and fire shall o'erthrow,
All whom war, death, age, agues, tyrannies,
Despair, law, chance, hath slain, and you whose eyes
Shall behold God, and never taste death's woe.

Christians hold that the relation of the resurrection body to the earthly body is one of continuity and transformation. In his first letter to the Corinthians the apostle Paul compares the human body to a seed that is transformed into a flower. It is sown in one condition, but it blooms forth in another—continuity but wonderful transformation.

The best illustration of the change is the risen Jesus. He was different. The two who walked the Emmaus Road with him did not recognize him. When he took bread to break it, however, he was known to them in this simple act (Lk 24:30-31).

Apparently, life in the world to come demands similar "spiritual bodies," personalities suited to a spiritual environment. Christian believers will not be mere shadows of their former selves, nor physical copies. They will be changed, transformed for life in heaven. As David Winter says in his book *Hereafter,* "Just as the caterpillar has to be changed into the butterfly in order to inherit the air, so we have to be changed in order to inherit heaven."

The Vindication of Justice

Christ's return will bring judgment as well as resurrection. The life to come demands not only transformed bodies but also the vindication of justice.

Few would deny that life in this world is unjust. The rich exploit the poor, the ruthless terrorize the humble and the powerful abuse the weak. Lovable children are denied a stable home, and capable couples are unable to have babies. Tyrants die peacefully in their beds, while saints sometimes pass in agony to the stake. Clearly, men and women know no universal justice on planet earth. The most massive injustices go unpunished, and the most admirable unselfishness goes unrewarded.

Yet the instinct of justice remains strong in all of us. One of the first things a child learns to say is "It's not fair." We spend our years appealing to some abstract principle of justice that we feel in our bones and assume that everyone else feels too. Nationality, politics and culture make no difference. Communists, atheists, humanists and Christians make the same appeal: "It's not fair." And yet we all recognize that, in the final analysis, this life is not fair. Even with the best intentions in the world, human justice is fallible.

How can a God who is almighty and good possibly allow this pervasive injustice to continue? If he does nothing, either now or after this life, to correct this gross unfairness and dethrone the reign of evil, either he is not all-powerful (and so cannot do it) or he is not good (and so does not care). But if he is all-powerful and good—which is what the word *God* means to most of us—then it seems he must act to put things right. Justice on a cosmic scale must prevail and must be seen to prevail, or God is not God.[3]

Obviously, God has not yet established justice on earth. So the strong presumption is that he will establish it after this life is over. And that is what the Bible teaches. Paul wrote the Thessalonians, "God is just: He will pay back trouble to those who trouble you and give relief to you who are troubled. . . . This will happen when the Lord Jesus is revealed from heaven in blazing fire with his powerful angels" (2 Thess 1:6-7).

The theme of the final judgment of God, in which the mighty are dethroned, the proud are scattered in the imagination of their hearts, the rich are sent away empty and the good who are hungry and poor are exalted, runs strongly through the teaching of Jesus and the apostles (Lk 1:51-53). We might think that God is blind to human injustice, but one day humankind will see that he cares intensely about it, and the inequalities and evils of life on earth will be put right.

Henry Wadsworth Longfellow affirmed the triumph of divine justice in those familiar lines about the meaning of Christmas:

I heard the bells on Christmas day
Their old familiar carols play,
And wild and sweet the words repeat
Of peace on earth, goodwill to men.

And in despair I bowed my head:
"There is no peace on earth," I said.
"For hate is strong, and mocks the song
Of peace on earth, goodwill to men."

Then pealed the bells more loud and deep:
"God is not dead, nor doth He sleep;
The wrong shall fail, the right prevail,
With peace on earth, goodwill to men."
("I Heard the Bells on Christmas Day")

Jesus described the final judgment in terms of a shepherd's separating sheep from goats (Mt 25:32). However much it may offend liberal sentiment, the Bible indicates that Jesus believed and taught that people could be excluded from the future life with God.

That negative note, however, is not the dominant theme of the New Testament or of the Christian faith. The resounding melody of the New Testament is not death and despair but life and hope. Christ has come and will come again. And that truth, Christians have always confessed, gives us reason to sing.

21

NEW DAY DAWNING

THE WORLD TO COME

Above the altar, at the far end of the Sistine Chapel in the Vatican, stands Michelangelo's massive painting *The Last Judgment.* High in the center of the scene sits Jesus Christ, his right arm raised in vigorous, decisive judgment of the earth's peoples. Below him, heavy figures of the condemned tumble uncontrollably downward toward the darkness of perdition, while the figures of the blessed sweep upward to join the angels in the realms of light.

The Christian vision of the world to come is so grand, so all-encompassing, so awe-inspiring that only a Michelangelo or a Dante or a Bunyan dares trace its boundaries for the human imagination. Human words simply fail and artistic genius falters when men and women contemplate the Christian vision of the life to come.

So when we ask what Christians believe about the life to come, we recognize the limitations of all human descriptions. Christians dare to speak only because God has revealed the reality. The Bible, they contend, teaches that the "life everlasting" is the fulfillment of God's work in time; it is the consummation of his purposes in creation.

Christians are not alone in their hope for a life to come. To masses of people, as we have seen, the finite world that impinges on our senses draws its existence from a realm of reality beyond itself. That is why peoples throughout history, and in non-Western nations in our own time, look at death with a strange blend of hope and dread.

Archaeologists, digging in the graves of people who lived ten thousand years ago, have found time and again some object that points to a crude conception of the afterlife: weapons for the happy hunting ground, or a canoe for crossing to the "isle of the blessed." But whatever the image, the afterlife is a central part of the religious faith. This life is but a prelude to the next.

The Ultimate Choice

The life to come is also central in Christianity. Early Christians stated it simply: "I believe in the life everlasting." But what do Christians expect to find in the life to come?

Unlike the other world religions, Christianity speaks of life after death with a note of certainty. We can trace this certainty, like so many others, to Jesus Christ. He taught his followers about the Hidden World because he said he came from there. And when his enemies hounded him to death, he arose from the realms of the dead and demonstrated to his disciples his right to speak of the invisible world and of the conditions that they could expect to find there.

As a consequence, Christians have always taught that men and women have only two fundamental alternatives before them. Either they have God—and in him everything eternal—or they have nothing but themselves. One is called heaven and the other hell. Human choices, arising from the Supreme Choice in this life, determine which it will be for eternity.

Jesus Christ indicated that every day, in a host of minute and major decisions, men and women choose death instead of life. They live in the kingdom of death instead of the Kingdom of God. His passion to deliver men and women from this spiritual darkness explains his single-minded purpose. He knew that if people did not repent of their sins and look to God for his undeserved forgiveness, they were already prisoners of hell.

Today it is no longer fashionable to speak of hell. Modern people have become so sensible, so wise in their own eyes, that any idea of judgment or hell is treated as nothing more than a stage for jokes.

Most people in Europe and the United States have been told so often that everyone has a spark of good within that they have come to believe that God will eventually welcome almost everyone to a blissful eternity. And even where people do not share this optimistic assessment of human nature, notions of hell are so widely ridiculed as to leave people with the impression that they can take their chances on life after death. "Live for the moment, don't worry about tomorrow."

It should be clear that more than outdated images of hell have been discarded in this secular faith. In rejecting the old images of eternity as grotesque and immoral people make the mistake of rejecting the truth. The Christian insight into the eternal significance of the decisions we make in this life has gone as well. Many no longer think of their daily decisions—is it right or wrong?—as anything other than daily decisions. Life is simply lived; it is no longer chosen. As a result, millions endure a largely meaningless day-to-day existence.

It's almost impossible to tell whether most people are rejecting some degraded presentation of the Christian faith or the faith itself. But so many people ridicule the traditional images that they compel thoughtful Christians to explain their language.

What can we say, then, about the crowns, the harps, the golden streets and the pearly gates in traditional descriptions of heaven? They are the biblical writer's way of suggesting to the imagination what cannot be put in prosaic terms. They are attempts to express the inexpressible. White robes are symbols of spotless purity, crowns point to moral victories, harps represent abounding happiness and gold suggest the timelessness of heaven. All these things—purity, moral victory, abounding happiness, permanence—are realities most people crave but cannot find on this earth.

Similar figurative language appears in the Bible when an author speaks of hell. Fire suggests suffering; darkness indicates isolation; a bottomless pit points to abject fear and insecurity. These, too, are experiences of men and women in this life, especially people who are enslaved to pleasure and pride and have no room for love in their lives. The language of hell, then, points not only to conditions beyond this life but also to conditions people can experience on this earth.

Consider the dilemma of the biblical authors. They are trying to describe conditions of existence that no one has fully fathomed. And yet they must draw upon experiences of people in this life to make the other world imaginable.

The Great Divorce
Relying on an assortment of images, Christianity has always taught the reality of hell as well as the exultation of heaven. The term *hell* is the translation of a Greek word in the New Testament, *gehenna,* meaning "valley of Hinnom." Since the second century B.C. the Jews believed that this valley south of Jerusalem—where child sacrifice had once taken place—would one day be the scene of judgment. Open flames would devour the godless. Christians adopted this Jewish word to indicate the destiny of unrepentant spiritual rebels.

Gehenna, however, is not the only term the New Testament uses to designate the destiny of the condemned. The idea also appears as everlasting fire, eternal wrath, outer darkness and "weeping and gnashing of teeth." This suggests that the New Testament is not so much interested in determining the *place* of hell as in indicating the *conditions* under which the condemned are destined to live.

This condemnation should strike no one as a sudden surprise. It is merely the fruit of a life cultivated in evil. In his *The Great Divorce* C. S. Lewis says the condemned are simply those to whom God finally says, "Your will be done."[1]

Non-Christians often ask the Christian, "But how can the God of love allow any of his creatures to suffer unending misery?" The real question is, how can he not?

The fact that God is love makes hell necessary. "Hell," E. L. Mascall once said, "is not compatible with God's love; it is a direct consequence of it."[2] That was his way of stressing the fact that the God who loves us is the God who respects our decisions. He loves us, but he does not force his love on us. To force love is to commit assault. He allows us to decide. He loves us, he encourages our response, he woos us, he pursues us, he urges us, but he does not force us, because he respects us.

God leaves the choice to us. Either we can throw ourselves in gratitude into the arms of self-existent Love, or we can repel it in a brutish attempt to affirm our own self-sufficiency. After all, what place could there be in a community throbbing with love for people concerned only to assert themselves?

In Jean-Paul Sartre's play *No Exit* three characters—Inez, Estelle and Garcin—find themselves together after death. All of them have died under circumstances that are clearly disgraceful.

In the room where the three are confined, it soon becomes obvious that each of them is interested in the others only as an audience for his or her own attempts at self-justification and displays of self-pity. None of them cares for the others for any other reason. None shows any sign of gratitude or penitence; all are resentful and bitter.

As the play proceeds, it becomes plain that these three persons are doomed to remain alone together throughout eternity. The unheeded arguments repeat themselves in endless circles, and the emotional tension becomes unbearable. No sympathy. No love. No community. As the curtain descends on the scene of never-ending and ever-mounting frustration, the inmates sum up the significance of the drama in two desperate exclamations: "We shall be together for ever! Hell is other people!"[3]

Significantly, on other lips these sentiments might be descriptions of the joys of heaven. "We shall be together for ever"—the communion of saints in the life everlasting.

The Grand Alternative
In describing heaven the Bible sometimes tells us how it is unlike our

present life, and sometimes how it is so much more than this life.

For example, in John's vision of heaven, found in the book of Revelation, he hears a loud voice from the throne: "God . . . will wipe every tear from their eyes. There will be no more death or mourning or crying or pain, for the old order of things has passed away" (Rev 21:4). Heaven is apparently sharply different from the sorrow-filled existence people find on earth. And that is part of its wonder.

The ancient book of Job says, "Man born of woman is of few days and full of trouble" (14:1). An African-American spiritual echoes this theme but adds the note of release:

> Soon we will be done wit' de troubles of de world,
>
> troubles of de world, troubles of de world.
>
> Soon we will be done wit' de troubles of de world.
>
> Goin' home to live with God.

Heaven is unlike earth. That is the point. In speaking of the presence of God, John apparently intended for us to turn sorrow and death and pain upside-down. Heaven, he suggests, will be filled with joy and life and pleasure.

John's vision of heaven, in fact, paints a whole series of contrasts with earth. In contrast to the darkness of most ancient cities, John says heaven is always lighted. In contrast to rampant disease in the ancient world, he says heaven has trees whose leaves heal all sorts of sicknesses. In contrast to the parched deserts of the Near East, he pictures heaven with an endless river of crystal-clear water. In contrast to a meager existence in an arid climate, John says twelve kinds of fruit grow on the trees of heaven. In a word, heaven is a wonderful destiny, free of the shortages and discomforts of this life.

But can we be more specific? How is heaven like life here and now?

The Vision of God

We find a clue in Jesus' beatitude: "Blessed are the pure in heart, for they will see God" (Mt 5:8). To see God is to live.

But what can it mean to see God? A moment's reflection will reveal that it is possible to "see" in several senses. A tourist might drive up to an observation point at the Grand Canyon and leave after half an hour. Has he seen the Grand Canyon? A traveler might fly in and out of the airport at Paris. Has she seen Paris? This is not what the Bible means when it promises that the pure in heart will see God.

There is, however, another type of sight. Have you ever noticed two lovers at a sidewalk café? They sit for hours, sipping a drink and staring into each other's eyes. They are lost in the wonder of each other. Their highest pleasure is to be with the lover. Surely this is closer to the meaning of "seeing" God. It is the contemplation, the magnetic beauty, the inner delight of basking in the presence of Someone you love.

The Bible makes clear, however, that human sight alone cannot bear the vision of God. When Moses, the leader with whom God spoke face to face, begged that God would show him his glory, God responded, "You cannot see my face, for no one may see me and live." So God told Moses: "There is a place near me where you may stand on a rock. When my glory passes by, I will put you in a cleft in the rock and cover you with my hand until I have passed by. Then I will remove my hand and you will see my back; but my face must not be seen" (Ex 33:18-23).

It is true that on occasion in the Old Testament God does appear to men and women. But when he does the note of terror always sounds. When Isaiah saw the Lord high and lifted up in the temple, he cried out: "Woe to me! I am ruined! . . . my eyes have seen the King, the LORD Almighty" (Is 6:5).

In a similar way, when God appeared to Ezekiel by the banks of the Chebar River, his glory was veiled. What Ezekiel saw was "the likeness as the appearance of a man" (Ezek 1:26 KJV). Even then, however, the prophet fell on his face in awe at the sight. The message seems clear: to see God is to die.

Something obviously had to be done. That is what the Christian gospel proclaims: God has done something. He has made possible the vision of God. "No one has ever seen God, but God the One and Only, who is at the Father's side, has made him known" (Jn 1:18). When Philip came to Jesus with the request "Lord, show us the Father,"

Jesus replied, "Anyone who has seen me has seen the Father" (Jn 14:8-9). Men and women see God, then, in Jesus Christ. That vision is possible now by faith. Heaven is a promise that someday it will be "face to face."

To "see" God in that sense means to love him, to praise him, to enjoy him. It is the end of our selfish search for happiness. It is the homecoming of the prodigal. It is the satisfaction of the thirst that we could not quench. It is the reason for our existence. It is the end of our creation. It is peace and home and rest. It is heaven.

Sometimes people ask, "Will you go to heaven when you die?" But a more important question is: "Are you the sort of person to whom heaven would seem desirable?" The choices we make in life are built up into our characters as bricks are built up into a house. They make us the kind of people we are.

G. B. Caird once said, "The man who habitually puts his trust in God and tries to follow in the steps of Jesus Christ will become the sort of person who would be at home in the presence of God. The man who laughs at the gospel, breaks all the rules, and throws away his life in unrepentant waste, will become the sort of person who would be more seriously out of place in heaven than a tone-deaf man in a roomful of musicians." The presence of God would be to such a person a worse torture than all the horrors of hell.[4]

That is why the Christian doctrines of heaven and hell are so much more than mere doctrines. They are reminders that every day in a host of ways we are all making choices—casting ballots, if you please—for the eternity that awaits us.

> Finish then thy new creation,
> Pure and spotless let us be;
> Let us see thy great salvation
> Perfectly restored in thee!
> Changed from glory into glory,
> Till in heav'n we take our place,
> Till we cast our crowns before thee,
> Lost in wonder, love, and praise![5]

Notes

Chapter 1: Lost in the Secular City

[1]Quoted in Louis Cassels, *The Reality of God* (Scottsdale, Pa.: Herald, 1972), p. 13.

[2]I am grateful to Harry Blamires for this point about twentieth-century novelists. See his *The Christian Mind* (Ann Arbor, Mich.: Servant, 1963), chap. 1.

[3]G. K. Chesterton, *Orthodoxy* (Glasgow: Collins, 1908), p. 53.

[4]G. B. Caird, *The Truth of the Gospel* (London: Oxford University Press, 1950), p. 110.

[5]C. S. Lewis, *An Anthology of C. S. Lewis,* ed. Clyde S. Kilby (New York: Harcourt, Brace & World, 1969), pp. 22, 24.

[6]J. B. Phillips, *The Newborn Christian* (New York: Macmillan, 1978), p. 140.

Chapter 2: We Are Not Alone

[1]Bertrand Russell, "A Free Man's Worship," in *The Basic Writings of Bertrand Russell,* ed. Robert E. Egner and Lester E. Dononn (New York: Simon & Schuster, 1961), p. 67.

[2]Martin Luther, *Lectures on Galatians,* in *Luther's Works,* ed. Jaroslav Pelikan (St. Louis: Concordia Publishing House, 1963), 26:399-400.

[3]Quoted in Lewis, *Anthology,* p. 23.

[4]C. S. Lewis, *Reflections on the Psalms* (New York: Harcourt, Brace & World, 1958), pp. 116-17.

Chapter 3: The Exodus and the Entrance

[1]The story of Bishop Felix is from Herbert Workman's *Persecution in the Early Church* (London: Epworth, 1923), p. 275.

Chapter 4: The Ranks of the Resistance

[1]Langdon Gilkey tells of his experience in his book *Shantung Compound* (New York: Harper & Row, 1966).

[2]Aleksandr I. Solzhenitsyn, *The Gulag Archipelago* (New York: Harper & Row, 1973), p. 168.

Chapter 5: Speaking Terms
[1] I have taken the Stevenson story from Cornelius Plantinga Jr., *A Place to Stand* (Grand Rapids, Mich.: Bible Way, 1981), p. 44.
[2] Chesterton, *Orthodoxy*, p. 31.
[3] C. S. Lewis, *Mere Christianity* (London: Collins, 1952), bk. 3, chap. 11.

Chapter 6: The Ultimate Ruler
[1] J. S. Whale, *Christian Doctrine* (London: Collins, 1963), p. 55.
[2] Quoted in Cassels, *The Reality of God*, p. 42.

Chapter 7: What Is God Like?
[1] The opening story of the battlefield is from Roger L. Shinn, *Life, Death and Destiny* (Philadelphia: Westminster Press, 1957), p. 9.
[2] Blaise Pascal *Pensées* 555.
[3] C. S. Lewis, *Letters to Malcolm: Chiefly on Prayer* (New York: Harcourt Brace Jovanovich, 1964), p. 75.
[4] Quoted in Thomas S. Kepler, ed., *Anthology of Devotional Literature* (Grand Rapids, Mich.: Baker Book House, 1947), p. 377.
[5] Norman Snaith, *The Distinctive Ideas of the Old Testament* (London: Epworth, 1944), p. 102.

Chapter 8: The Dark Side of Life
[1] The quotations from Charles Templeton are in a news story by George W. Cornell in *The Denver Post*, May 19, 1978.
[2] Peter Berger's observation is quoted in Cassels, *The Reality of God*, p. 14.
[3] Quoted in Cassels, *The Reality of God*, p. 31.
[4] Lewis, *Mere Christianity*, bk. 2, chap. 1.
[5] I first saw the argument about the "scale of evil" in E. L. Mascall, *The Christian Universe* (New York: Morehouse-Barlow, 1966), p. 151.

Chapter 9: The Invasion
[1] Lewis, *Mere Christianity*, bk. 2, chap. 3. Used by permission of the original publisher, William Collins Sons, London.
[2] Dorothy L. Sayers, *Creed or Chaos?* (New York: Harcourt Brace, 1949), p. 24.
[3] Michael Green, ed., *The Truth of God Incarnate* (Grand Rapids, Mich.: Eerdmans, 1977), p. 26.
[4] See Henry Bettenson, ed., *Documents of the Christian Church* (New York: Oxford University Press, 1943), pp. 69-72.
[5] See Whale, *Christian Doctrine*, p. 102.

Chapter 10: The Agony and the Answer
[1] C. S. Lewis, *The Lion, the Witch and the Wardrobe* (Middlesex, U.K.: Puffin Books, 1950), p. 148.

[2]Harry Blamires, *On Christian Truth* (Ann Arbor, Mich.: Servant, 1983), p. 52.
[3]I have drawn the argument about psychic phenomena from Green, *The Truth of God Incarnate,* pp. 54-55.
[4]The argument about the resurrection as a "hoax" is from Caird, *The Truth of the Gospel,* p. 86.
[5]James D. Smart, *The ABC's of the Christian Faith* (Philadelphia: Westminster Press, 1968), p. 46.

Chapter 12: Whispers of the Wind
[1]J. A. Findlay, *A Portrait of Paul* (London: Epworth, 1936), p. 102.

Chapter 13: God in Three Persons
[1]Dorothy Sayers uses this analogy of creativity in a very insightful discussion of the doctrine of the Trinity. See her book *The Mind of the Maker* (New York: Harper & Row, 1941).
[2]See Leonard Hodgson, *The Doctrine of the Trinity* (London: Nisbet, 1943), pp. 50, 59.

Chapter 14: New People
[1]Mike Yaconelli, *Tough Faith* (Elgin, Ill.: David C. Cook, 1976), p. 31.
[2]The position I take in this chapter, stressing the church as a community of faith, is akin to the evangelical tradition rooted in the Protestant Reformation of the sixteenth century. Many other Christians hold the "catholic" position, which stresses the essential role of a divinely appointed priesthood in defining the church.

Chapter 15: The Basic Steps
[1]The reader needs to note the way I have raised the question. The Bible, the message preached and the sacraments are ways the Word—the revelation of God—comes to us. Obviously there are distinctions between the "forms" of the Word. First, God revealed himself in special actions and words in history. Then, under the Spirit's guidance, prophets and apostles wrote it down. Finally, the church listens to the Word and teaches it today. The priority here is important. See Shirley C. Guthrie Jr., *Christian Doctrine* (Richmond, Va.: Covenant Life, 1968), pp. 80-82.
[2]Elton Trueblood's comparison of fire and evangelism is in his book *The Incendiary Fellowship* (New York: Harper & Row, 1967).

Chapter 16: Forgiven Sinners
[1]Kate B. Wilkinson, "May the Mind of Christ, My Savior." Used by permission.
[2]Lewis, *Mere Christianity,* bk. 4, chap. 8.
[3]The Payton incident is found in A. Bernard Webber, *More Illustrations and Quotable Poems* (Grand Rapids, Mich.: Zondervan, 1945), p. 47.

Chapter 17: The Family Likeness
[1]The Jonathan Edwards quotation can be found in Hugh T. Kerr and John M. Mulder,

eds., *Conversions* (Grand Rapids, Mich.: Eerdmans, 1983), p. 69.

[2]Adolf Deissmann discusses this concept in his book *Saint Paul: A Study in Social and Religious History* (London: Hodder & Stoughton, 1926), pp. 140-57.

[3]I found these lines in A. M. Hunter, *Taking the Christian View* (Atlanta: John Knox Press, 1974), p. 83.

Chapter 18: The Difference Faith Makes

[1]Many of the ideas in the sections "Ideals of the Western World" and "Light in the Darkness" came originally from Caird, *The Truth of the Gospel,* pp. 150-62.

[2]I have drawn the argument about care of children and slaves from John Foster's fine article "Achievements of Christ in Twenty Centuries," in *The Coming-of-Age of Christianity,* ed. Sir James Marchant (Westport, Conn.: Greenwood, 1971), pp. 1ff.

[3]I am indebted to G. B. Caird for the analogy of Roman colonies and the church in society. It is found in *The Truth of the Gospel,* pp. 159-62.

Chapter 19: The Point of Providence

[1]The address by Malcolm Muggeridge is found in *Let the Earth Hear His Voice* (Minneapolis: World Wide, 1975), pp. 449-56.

[2]Quoted in Roger L. Shinn, *Christianity and the Problem of History* (New York: Scribner's, 1953), p. 4.

[3] Herbert Butterfield, *Christianity and History* (London: G. Bell and Sons, 1954), p. 94.

[4]Quoted in Shinn, *Christianity and the Problem of History,* p. 77.

[5]Augustine *The City of God* 1. 29.

[6]Christopher Dawson, *The Kingdom of God and History* (New York: Willett, Clark, 1938), p. 138.

Chapter 20: The Final Curtain

[1]Shinn, *Life, Death and Destiny,* pp. 84-85.

[2]Hunter, *Taking the Christian View,* p. 58.

[3]This argument is drawn from David Winter, *Hereafter* (Wheaton, Ill.: Harold Shaw, 1972), pp. 82-85.

Chapter 21: New Day Dawning

[1]C. S. Lewis, *The Great Divorce* (New York: Macmillan, 1946), p. 72.

[2]Mascall, *Christian Universe,* p. 148.

[3]Jean-Paul Sartre, *No Exit and Three Other Plays* (New York: Random House, 1955).

[4]Caird, *The Truth of the Gospel,* p. 126.

[5]Charles Wesley, "Love Divine, All Loves Excelling."

Printed in the United States
35109LVS00002B/166-183